LA PA
TRAVEL

2025 & 2026 Practical Companion For Exploring The Most Northwesterly Island Of The Canary Islands Like A Local Featuring Expert Insights And Illustrated Map

BEVERLY MACKLIN

Copyright © 2025 by Beverly Macklin
All rights reserved.

No portion of this publication may be reproduced, stored in a retrieval system, or transmitted in any form or by any means—whether electronic, mechanical, photocopying, recording, or otherwise—without the prior written consent of the author, except for brief quotations included in reviews or other noncommercial uses permitted under copyright law.

This book is an original work of nonfiction. While every effort has been made to ensure the accuracy of the information contained within, the author cannot accept responsibility for any loss, injury, or inconvenience resulting from its use.

Printed in the United States of America

About The Author

Beverly Macklin is a travel writer, storyteller, and keen observer of culture, drawn to hidden paths and the untold stories that linger behind every winding road, quiet village, and bustling street. With a deep respect for local traditions and an attentive eye for practical advice, Beverly creates travel guides that transcend mere itineraries—they invite readers into a journey of understanding, connection, and shared curiosity.

From misty Nordic fjords to sunlit Mediterranean harbors, Beverly's travels are grounded in firsthand experience and fueled by a desire to help others explore thoughtfully and meaningfully. Each guide embodies a dedication to responsible tourism, environmental consciousness, and the belief that real travel is less about ticking off places on a map and more about engaging with people, savoring the moment, and embracing the unexpected.

When not charting new routes or chatting with locals in hidden cafés, Beverly can often be found on solitary hikes, scribbling reflections in well-worn notebooks, or planning her next adventure off the beaten path.

TABLE OF CONTENTS

MAP 6
Chapter 1 7
Welcome to La Palma 7
    Discovering the Island 7
    A First Glimpse of La Palma 11
    Essential Facts 16
Chapter 2 22
Getting There 22
    Flights and Connections 22
    Arriving by Sea 27
    Transfers and Transport 32
Chapter 3 38
First Impressions 38
    The Island's Charm 38
    Sights that Impress 43
    Settling In 48
Chapter 4 53
Where to Stay 53
    Hotels and Resorts 53
    Charming Guesthouses 58
    Unique Stays 63
Chapter 5 68
Adventures 68
    Hiking Trails and Volcano Tours 68
    Water Sports and Beaches 73
    Exploring the Natural Wonders 77

Chapter 6 83
Local Flavors 83
   Must-Try Dishes 83
   Cafes and Markets 88
   Sweet Treats 92
Chapter 7 97
Island Life 97
   Villages and Towns 97
   Daily Routines 102
   Festivals and Local Events 106
Chapter 8 112
Hidden Gems 112
   Secret Viewpoints 112
   Off-the-Beaten-Path Spots 117
   Local Stories 121
Chapter 9 127
Shopping & Souvenirs 127
   Markets and Boutiques 127
   Handmade Treasures 132
   What to Bring Home 136
Chapter 10 141
Practical Tips 141
   Safety and Health 141
   Money Matters 145
   Travel Essentials 150
Chapter 11 155
Saying Goodbye 155
   Last Experiences 155

Capturing Memories 159
Planning Your Return 163

MAP

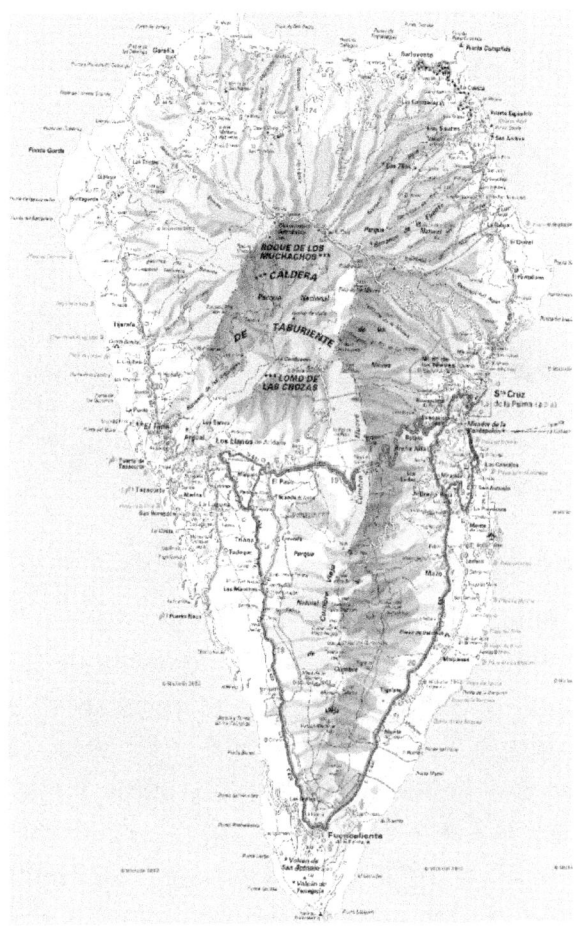

Chapter 1

Welcome to La Palma

Discovering the Island

La Palma, often called "La Isla Bonita" or "The Beautiful Island," is the most northwestern of the Canary Islands. Its striking landscapes, lush greenery, volcanic terrain, and star-studded skies make it a destination unlike any other. While the Canary Islands are known for their warm climate and beaches, La Palma offers a quieter, more intimate experience for travelers seeking natural beauty, adventure, and a connection with nature. Exploring La Palma is like stepping into a living postcard: verdant forests, volcanic craters, dramatic cliffs, and picturesque villages unfold around every corner.

The island is roughly 708 square kilometers, small enough to explore comfortably within a week or two, yet large enough to offer a variety of environments. Its geography is defined by steep mountains, deep ravines, and the famous Caldera de Taburiente, a massive volcanic crater that dominates the island's central region. La Palma is a volcanic island formed millions of years ago, and its terrain is still very much alive. The lava flows, black sand beaches, and rugged cliffs remind visitors of the island's dramatic geological history.

La Palma's history is deeply intertwined with the indigenous Guanches, the first inhabitants of the Canary Islands. Their legacy remains visible in archaeological sites, traditional crafts, and local customs. Spanish colonization in the 15th century added layers of culture, architecture, and agriculture, leaving behind quaint villages with cobbled streets, whitewashed houses, and charming town squares. Wandering through towns like Santa Cruz de La Palma or Los Llanos gives a sense of the island's rich cultural tapestry.

One of La Palma's most captivating features is its biodiversity. The island's forests, particularly the laurel forests in the north, are home to endemic species of plants and birds found nowhere else on Earth. Walking through these forests feels like entering a prehistoric world, with moss-covered trees, misty trails, and the melodic sounds of birds filling the air. The island's volcanic slopes are also home to unique flora that has adapted to the rocky terrain, adding a striking contrast of life amidst the lava and ash.

La Palma is not just for nature lovers; it has earned the designation of a Starlight Reserve, recognized internationally for its exceptionally clear night skies. The island is home to some of the best astronomical observatories in the world. Visitors often find themselves gazing at the Milky Way, planets, and distant galaxies with an astonishing clarity, especially from locations like Roque de los Muchachos. Nighttime on La Palma is a magical experience, where the celestial show complements the island's natural beauty.

For those drawn to adventure, La Palma offers endless possibilities. Hiking, cycling, and water sports are abundant. Trails traverse volcanic landscapes, coastal paths, and dense forests. Kayaking along the island's dramatic coastline or diving into its crystal-clear waters reveals a world of marine life, including colorful fish, rays, and occasionally dolphins. The combination of adventure and serenity is one of La Palma's most alluring traits.

La Palma's culture is vibrant yet unassuming. Festivals such as the Bajada de la Virgen de las Nieves, celebrated every five years, showcase traditional music, dance, and religious ceremonies. Music and folklore are woven into everyday life, and the island's residents take pride in maintaining traditions that have been passed down through generations. Visiting local markets, artisan shops, or participating in a village fiesta allows travelers to experience the island's authentic spirit.

Culinary experiences on La Palma are deeply connected to its land and sea. The island's fertile soils produce excellent potatoes, bananas, and tropical fruits, while its waters provide fresh fish and seafood. Traditional dishes like "mojo" sauces, papas arrugadas (wrinkled potatoes), and fresh grilled fish highlight simple, fresh ingredients with bold flavors. Sampling local wines, particularly from the volcanic vineyards, adds another dimension to the island's sensory appeal.

Transportation around La Palma is relatively straightforward, though the island's mountainous terrain means winding roads and varying elevations. Renting a car is often recommended for full exploration, allowing visitors to reach secluded viewpoints, hidden beaches, and remote hiking trails. For those preferring public transport, buses connect major towns and tourist spots, though schedules can be less frequent in rural areas.

Discovering La Palma is an invitation to slow down and immerse oneself in nature, culture, and adventure. It is an island that rewards curiosity: the more you explore, the more layers of beauty and history reveal themselves. Each visit leaves a lasting impression, and it is easy to understand why travelers return again and again, captivated by the island's unique charm.

Whether you are walking through misty laurel forests, climbing volcanic peaks, savoring local cuisine, or simply watching the stars, La Palma offers a profound sense of wonder and discovery. It is a place where every turn brings new surprises, every moment invites reflection, and every experience becomes a cherished memory.

A First Glimpse of La Palma

Stepping onto La Palma for the first time is an experience that instantly captures the imagination. Whether arriving by plane at the small but efficient La Palma Airport or by ferry docking along the island's rugged coastline, travelers are immediately greeted by an island that feels both intimate and dramatic. The first view is often of steep mountains rising sharply from the ocean, lush forests blanketing their slopes, and the sparkling Atlantic surrounding the island. Unlike larger, busier destinations, La Palma offers a sense of calm and personal connection; the island seems to welcome each visitor with quiet grandeur.

The approach from the air is particularly striking. As the plane descends, travelers can see the patchwork of green forests, volcanic craters, and terraced fields that hint at the island's agricultural heritage. Coastal cliffs plunge into deep blue waters, while small villages with red-tiled roofs dot the hillsides. From above, La Palma's topography is revealed in all its complexity: valleys carved over millennia, volcanic cones scattered across the terrain, and the iconic Caldera de Taburiente dominating the central highlands. For first-time visitors, this aerial view provides a sense of the island's scale, diversity, and natural drama.

Upon landing, the sensory experience continues. The air feels fresher than in most tourist destinations, carrying hints of salt from the sea, the earthy aroma of volcanic soil, and the subtle fragrance of tropical and subtropical plants. Even a brief walk from the airport or port into nearby towns introduces travelers to the island's charm: cobbled streets, whitewashed buildings, colorful shutters, and flowering balconies create a visual feast. The slower pace of life is immediately noticeable, offering a refreshing contrast to the hustle of larger tourist hubs.

Santa Cruz de La Palma, the island's capital, often serves as the first destination for many visitors. This coastal town provides a glimpse into La Palma's colonial history with its narrow streets, elegant balconies, and plazas surrounded by historic buildings. The waterfront promenade invites a leisurely stroll, and the scent of fresh seafood from nearby restaurants hints at the culinary delights to come. The town's mixture of history, culture, and vibrant street life offers travelers their first intimate taste of island living.

Los Llanos de Aridane, the island's largest inland town, provides a different perspective. Here, modern life blends with traditional elements, giving travelers insight into everyday La Palma. Markets overflow with fresh fruits, vegetables, and artisan goods, while cafes invite visitors to pause and observe local routines. The contrast between the coastal calm of Santa Cruz and the lively streets of Los Llanos highlights the diversity of experiences on the island, even within a relatively small area.

The island's natural scenery continues to impress at the very first glimpse of its beaches and coastline.

Unlike many other Canary Islands, La Palma's beaches are often smaller, dramatic, and volcanic, with black sand and pebble shores bordered by cliffs and pine forests. Playa de Puerto Naos and Playa de Tazacorte are popular starting points for newcomers, offering calm waters, breathtaking sunsets, and the occasional glimpse of local wildlife. The combination of ocean, cliffs, and greenery is unique and provides an almost cinematic first impression.

Even casual travelers notice the island's volcanic heritage immediately. Lava flows and volcanic rocks are visible along roadsides, trails, and beaches, telling a story of creation and change. The landscape constantly reminds visitors that they are on a young, dynamic island shaped by fire and time. This sense of living geography makes La Palma distinct from other destinations, giving first-time explorers a sense of awe and curiosity.

Another element of La Palma's first impression is the sky. Often clear, bright, and intensely blue, it contrasts beautifully with the lush green forests and the deep ocean. In higher elevations, clouds may drift lazily below mountaintops, creating a dramatic "island in the clouds" effect. Observing this from viewpoints like Mirador de la Cumbrecita or the rim of the Caldera de Taburiente, even briefly, leaves visitors with an unforgettable sense of scale and wonder.

The locals contribute significantly to a traveler's first experience. Warm, friendly, and genuinely welcoming, they offer guidance, recommendations, and hospitality. Whether in small villages or towns, interactions with residents—whether in shops, cafes, or on hiking trails—provide context to the island's culture, values, and daily rhythms. First impressions are often shaped as much by these human interactions as by the natural and architectural scenery.

For many visitors, the first glimpse of La Palma is just a beginning. It sparks a desire to explore further, from hidden valleys and volcanic peaks to secluded beaches and charming towns. The initial visual, sensory, and cultural impressions plant the seed of curiosity that drives travelers to delve deeper into what makes La Palma extraordinary. Even a brief stay leaves a lasting memory of a place that is vibrant, serene, and remarkably diverse.

Ultimately, seeing La Palma for the first time is more than just arriving on an island—it is an introduction to a world of contrasts: rugged yet serene, lively yet tranquil, ancient yet evolving. Every glance at its mountains, valleys, towns, and coastline tells a story waiting to be discovered. The island's ability to surprise, charm, and inspire in those first moments sets the tone for the journey ahead, ensuring that visitors begin their adventure with a profound sense of anticipation and wonder.

Essential Facts

La Palma, the "Beautiful Island," is a destination that balances breathtaking natural beauty with accessible travel experiences, making it a must-visit location in the Canary Islands. For first-time visitors, understanding the essential facts about the island provides the foundation needed to make the most of a trip. Geography, climate, culture, history, transportation, and local customs all play a role in shaping a seamless and enjoyable journey. La Palma is roughly 708 square kilometers in size, making it one of the smaller Canary Islands, yet its compact nature allows travelers to explore a surprising range of landscapes—from verdant forests and volcanic craters to rugged cliffs and black sand beaches.

The island's population is around 85,000 residents, with most people concentrated in towns like Santa Cruz de La Palma, the capital, and Los Llanos de Aridane, the largest urban area. Despite its relatively small population, the island boasts a rich cultural life, with local festivals, traditional music, and artisan crafts reflecting centuries of history. La Palma's culture is a blend of indigenous Guanche heritage and Spanish colonial influence, visible in its architecture, town layouts, and community traditions. Walking through its villages and towns reveals a connection between past and present that is rarely seen in larger, more commercialized destinations.

La Palma's volcanic origins shape much of its geography. The Caldera de Taburiente, a massive volcanic crater at the island's center, dominates its landscape, offering trails for hikers of all levels and spectacular viewpoints. The island also features volcanic cones, lava fields, and ravines carved over millennia. These formations are not only visually striking but also provide insight into La Palma's geological history and ongoing volcanic activity. The volcanic soil is fertile, supporting agriculture, particularly banana plantations, vineyards, and other crops, which in turn influence the island's cuisine and local markets.

The climate on La Palma is generally mild year-round, making it suitable for travel at almost any season. Coastal areas experience warm temperatures, averaging 20–26°C (68–79°F) during the day, while higher elevations can be cooler, especially at night. Rainfall is concentrated in the winter months, primarily affecting the northern and central parts of the island, which contribute to the lush vegetation. The trade winds influence the microclimates, creating different environmental conditions within short distances—a unique feature that allows for diverse outdoor activities and sightseeing options.

Transport on the island is manageable but requires some planning. La Palma Airport, located near Santa Cruz de La Palma, connects the island with other Canary Islands and major European cities. Ferries provide an alternative route, linking La Palma with Tenerife and other islands. Renting a car is highly recommended for those wanting to explore remote locations, hike trails, or visit secluded viewpoints. Public transport is available in towns and for reaching some tourist destinations, but schedules may be less frequent in rural areas. Roads are generally well-maintained, although steep inclines and winding routes are common in mountainous regions.

For communications, La Palma is well-equipped. Mobile networks and internet connectivity are reliable in most towns and tourist areas, though some remote hiking trails or higher elevations may have limited coverage. Spanish is the official language, but English is widely understood in hotels, restaurants, and tourist services, making navigation and communication easier for international travelers. Currency is the Euro, and most businesses accept credit cards, although smaller shops and markets may operate primarily with cash.

Safety on La Palma is generally high. The island experiences low crime rates, and emergency services are accessible throughout the territory. Natural hazards are limited, though visitors should be aware of the volcanic terrain when hiking or exploring coastal cliffs. It is advisable to follow local guidance for outdoor activities, check weather forecasts for mountainous areas, and use proper footwear and equipment for trails. Health services are available in towns and hospitals, and travel insurance is recommended for peace of mind.

La Palma's gastronomy reflects its fertile lands and surrounding ocean. Fresh seafood, tropical fruits, and locally grown vegetables form the backbone of island cuisine. Traditional dishes include papas arrugadas with mojo sauces, fresh grilled fish, stews, and pastries. The island also produces excellent wines, many grown in volcanic soil that gives them unique flavors. Visitors can enjoy these culinary offerings at local restaurants, markets, and even vineyard tours, which provide both tasting experiences and insights into traditional agricultural practices.

Tourist services are well-developed despite the island's smaller size. Accommodation options range from boutique hotels and guesthouses to rural cottages and luxury resorts. Activities for visitors include hiking, cycling, stargazing, water sports, cultural tours, and scenic drives. La Palma is also recognized for its Starlight Reserve status, attracting amateur and professional astronomers to its observatories and clear night skies. This unique feature enhances both daytime exploration and nighttime experiences, adding an extra dimension to a visit.

Understanding these essential facts equips travelers with the knowledge needed to plan and enjoy their journey to La Palma. From climate and transportation to culture, cuisine, and geography, these details provide a practical foundation that enhances the overall experience. By grasping the basics, visitors can navigate the island with confidence, appreciate its unique characteristics, and discover its hidden treasures in a more meaningful way.

La Palma is more than just a travel destination; it is a place where natural beauty, rich history, and vibrant culture converge. Knowing the essential facts before arrival allows travelers to connect more deeply with the island, make informed choices, and savor every moment of their visit. From the mountains to the sea, from local traditions to modern comforts, these details form the framework for a journey filled with discovery, adventure, and lasting memories.

Chapter 2

Getting There

Flights and Connections

Arriving on La Palma is the first step in a journey that promises both tranquility and adventure. The island is accessible primarily by air, and its small but efficient airport, La Palma Airport (SPC), is the gateway for most visitors. Located just a few kilometers south of Santa Cruz de La Palma, the airport is strategically positioned to provide easy access to the island's towns, beaches, and mountainous regions. For first-time visitors, understanding the flight options, airlines, and travel logistics is crucial to a smooth arrival and sets the tone for a worry-free exploration of La Palma.

La Palma Airport connects the island with other Canary Islands, mainland Spain, and select international destinations, primarily in Europe. Flights from Tenerife, Gran Canaria, and Lanzarote are frequent, allowing travelers to combine islands in a single trip or use La Palma as a peaceful retreat after visiting more crowded destinations. Regular domestic flights from Madrid and Barcelona make La Palma accessible to travelers from mainland Spain, often serving as the most convenient route for international visitors arriving from other parts of the world. Seasonal charter flights also operate from various European cities, particularly during peak travel periods like summer and winter holidays.

Most travelers arriving from outside Spain will connect through Tenerife, Gran Canaria, or Madrid. For instance, a visitor from London might fly directly to Tenerife and then take a short connecting flight to La Palma, which typically lasts around 30 to 40 minutes. This makes La Palma highly accessible despite its small size and remote location. The island's airport is modern and efficient, with clear signage, rental car services, taxis, and shuttle options readily available, allowing travelers to move seamlessly from the runway to their accommodations or first sightseeing destinations.

Flight frequency can vary depending on the season, with summer and winter holidays offering the most options for international travelers. During these peak times, airlines may increase services, including charter flights, making it easier to find direct connections. In contrast, off-peak seasons might require travelers to schedule connecting flights through Tenerife or Gran Canaria, but these connections are generally straightforward and reliable. Booking in advance is recommended, especially for those traveling during busy holiday periods, to ensure the best availability and prices.

La Palma Airport is well-equipped for international travelers. Facilities include car rental counters, luggage services, cafes, and basic shopping options. While the airport is smaller compared to major European hubs, it efficiently handles the volume of tourists visiting the island and maintains a relaxed, organized atmosphere. Arrival procedures are typically quick, with immigration and customs processes streamlined for visitors from the European Union, and friendly staff available to assist those unfamiliar with the airport or the island.

For those considering ferry travel as an alternative or complement to flights, La Palma is accessible by sea from Tenerife and other nearby islands. Ferry services offer a slower, scenic option for those who wish to experience the Atlantic crossing and admire the islands from the water. While ferries are less commonly used than flights for first-time visitors, they are popular among locals, cyclists, and travelers transporting vehicles. Timetables vary depending on weather conditions, season, and demand, so it is essential to plan ahead and confirm schedules before departure.

Travelers should also consider the convenience of combining flights and ferries for a multi-island experience. Many visitors enjoy exploring the Canaries in stages, starting on La Palma and then visiting Tenerife, Gran Canaria, or La Gomera. Coordinating flights with ferries can extend the adventure, offering a unique perspective on the islands' geography, culture, and coastal scenery. These inter-island connections also allow for greater flexibility in planning itineraries, particularly for those who want to balance adventure with relaxation.

Airlines operating flights to La Palma include both full-service carriers and low-cost options. Domestic airlines like Binter Canarias and Canaryfly dominate inter-island routes, offering frequent, reliable service. International carriers, particularly from Germany, the United Kingdom, and mainland Spain, provide seasonal flights that connect La Palma with major European cities. For travelers seeking convenience and flexibility, low-cost carriers often present attractive options, while full-service airlines may include additional amenities such as checked luggage, onboard refreshments, and flexible booking policies.

Travelers arriving on La Palma should also be aware of luggage allowances, airport transfers, and rental car options. Many visitors choose to rent a car upon arrival to maximize exploration, as public transportation, while available, may not reach more remote hiking trails, viewpoints, or hidden beaches. Rental services at the airport are well-staffed, and reservations can be made in advance to ensure availability, particularly during high season. Taxis and shuttles are also available, offering direct connections to hotels or town centers.

Understanding flight options and connections is essential for a stress-free start to a La Palma adventure. Careful planning ensures travelers arrive ready to explore the island's lush forests, volcanic landscapes, dramatic coastline, and charming towns without worrying about logistics. Whether flying directly from Europe, connecting through another Canary Island, or even combining flights with a scenic ferry journey, the process is straightforward and designed to welcome visitors efficiently and comfortably.

By familiarizing oneself with these flight and connection essentials, travelers can focus on the excitement of arrival, knowing that the journey to La Palma is both manageable and enjoyable. The island's accessibility, combined with its unique landscapes and cultural richness, ensures that the moment of first landing is the perfect introduction to an unforgettable travel experience.

Arriving by Sea

Arriving on La Palma by sea offers a completely different experience compared to flying. While the island's airport provides quick and convenient access, the maritime approach immerses travelers in the dramatic beauty of the Atlantic and the island's rugged coastline, creating a sense of anticipation long before the ferry docks. Ferries connect La Palma with Tenerife, the neighboring Canary Islands, and occasionally other ports depending on the season, offering both practical transport and a scenic adventure for those who want to travel at a slower pace and enjoy the views from the water.

The main ferry terminals on La Palma are located in Santa Cruz de La Palma and Puerto Tazacorte. Santa Cruz de La Palma, the capital, is the primary hub for passenger ferries arriving from Tenerife and other islands. The harbor is well-equipped with passenger facilities, including ticket offices, waiting areas, and basic amenities such as cafes and restrooms. Upon approaching the port, travelers are greeted with sweeping views of the town's colonial architecture, the surrounding hills, and the ocean stretching toward the horizon, giving an immediate sense of the island's charm and character.

Ferry services to La Palma are operated by a number of companies, with Naviera Armas and Fred. Olsen Express being the most prominent. The duration of the journey depends on the point of departure and the type of vessel used. From Tenerife, the crossing typically takes around two to three hours on a conventional ferry, while high-speed catamarans may complete the trip in just over an hour. Travelers often find the slower ferries appealing because they allow for a relaxed journey, with time to enjoy the sea breeze, watch the cliffs approach, and observe marine life along the way.

One of the highlights of arriving by sea is the chance to see La Palma's dramatic coastline up close. The island's cliffs rise steeply from the Atlantic, with volcanic rocks and lush vegetation creating a striking contrast. Small coves and beaches, often hidden from view on land, become visible only from the water. This perspective offers a sense of the island's scale and rugged beauty that is impossible to replicate from the air. Photographers and nature enthusiasts, in particular, appreciate this approach, as it provides unique opportunities to capture La Palma's natural grandeur.

Travelers should note that ferry schedules are influenced by weather conditions, particularly wind and sea state. Rough seas can lead to delays or cancellations, so it is important to check the weather forecast and ferry operator announcements in advance. Seasonal variations also affect the frequency of service, with more crossings offered during the summer holiday months and fewer in the quieter winter season. Planning ahead is essential for coordinating ferry arrivals with accommodations, car rentals, or onward travel plans.

Boarding a ferry is straightforward, with vehicles and passengers typically separated for convenience. For those traveling with a car, the ferries provide ample space, making it easy to continue exploring the island immediately upon arrival. Passengers without vehicles can relax on deck or in comfortable seating areas, enjoying panoramic views of the approaching cliffs, volcanic formations, and shimmering Atlantic waters. Many ferries offer onboard services such as cafes, snack bars, and observation decks, allowing travelers to settle in and take in the scenery during the crossing.

For first-time visitors, arriving by sea also offers a more immersive sense of La Palma's culture and daily life. Local ferry routes are used not only by tourists but also by residents commuting between islands or transporting goods. Observing the interactions on board provides insight into the rhythms of island life and the practical connections between the Canary Islands. It also gives travelers a sense of being part of the local community, even for a brief moment.

Upon disembarking, the immediate impression is one of accessibility and friendliness. Ferry terminals are typically located close to town centers, making it easy to reach accommodations, rental cars, or sightseeing points without long transfers. Santa Cruz de La Palma's port, for instance, is within walking distance of historical streets, plazas, and cafes, allowing travelers to start exploring almost immediately. The contrast between the sea journey and arrival on land enhances the sense of discovery and transition from travel to immersion in the island environment.

Arriving by sea can also appeal to travelers seeking sustainability and a slower pace of travel. While flying offers speed, ferries provide a more environmentally conscious option, with lower carbon emissions per passenger. Additionally, the journey itself becomes part of the adventure, offering time to relax, reflect, and appreciate the Atlantic vistas. Many travelers find that the ferry arrival, with its gradual reveal of La Palma's cliffs and coastal scenery, creates a more memorable first impression than a quick flight descent.

In addition to practical transport, ferries sometimes include opportunities for sightseeing or even whale and dolphin watching. The waters around La Palma are home to diverse marine life, and attentive travelers may spot pods of dolphins, whales, or seabirds along the route. This natural spectacle enhances the journey, turning what could be a simple transfer into an experience in its own right. Travelers arriving by sea often recount the sense of anticipation and awe that builds as the island grows larger with each passing wave.

Overall, arriving on La Palma by sea combines practicality, scenery, and a touch of adventure. Whether traveling with a vehicle, on foot, or simply seeking a leisurely connection from another Canary Island, the ferry approach allows visitors to appreciate the island's unique coastal geography, enjoy panoramic views, and experience a more intimate introduction to the island. For those who choose this route, the journey itself becomes an integral part of the La Palma experience, setting the stage for the exploration, relaxation, and discoveries that await on land.

Transfers and Transport

Once you have arrived on La Palma, whether by plane or ferry, understanding the island's transport options is key to making the most of your stay. La Palma is compact enough that major towns and attractions are within reasonable driving distances, yet its mountainous terrain and winding coastal roads require careful planning. Transfers and transport are essential not only for convenience but also for accessing the island's hidden corners, scenic viewpoints, and natural wonders that make La Palma so special.

For many travelers, renting a car is the most practical and flexible way to explore the island. Car rental services are readily available at La Palma Airport, ferry terminals, and in larger towns like Santa Cruz de La Palma and Los Llanos de Aridane. Driving allows visitors to set their own pace, stop at viewpoints, and reach remote hiking trails or beaches that public transport does not serve. Roads are generally well-maintained, but the mountainous topography results in steep inclines, narrow bends, and occasionally sharp turns, so caution is advised, especially for those unfamiliar with such driving conditions.

For those who prefer not to drive, taxis provide a convenient alternative for short transfers or day trips. Taxis are readily available in towns, at airports, and ferry ports, and many can be booked in advance. Fares are generally reasonable, but longer journeys across the island's hills can add up quickly. It's a good idea to confirm prices before traveling, especially for longer trips or late-night rides. Taxis are also a practical option for visitors carrying luggage or traveling with small groups who want comfort without the responsibility of driving.

Public buses operate throughout La Palma and are an economical option for reaching major towns and tourist areas. The island's bus network connects Santa Cruz de La Palma, Los Llanos de Aridane, and smaller villages, offering routes to beaches, natural parks, and some viewpoints. While buses are reliable for routine travel, they can be less frequent on weekends or in remote areas, and schedules may change seasonally. Travelers relying on public transport should plan ahead and check timetables carefully to ensure smooth connections, particularly if they wish to catch a ferry or coordinate with guided tours.

For longer distances, especially those involving mountainous terrain, organized transfers or guided tours can be an excellent choice. Many hotels, resorts, and tour operators offer shuttle services to popular destinations such as the Caldera de Taburiente, Roque de los Muchachos, and scenic coastal drives. These services provide the convenience of local knowledge, safety, and efficiency, ensuring travelers reach their destinations without navigating unfamiliar roads. Guided tours often combine transport with expert commentary, enriching the experience with historical, geological, and cultural insights.

Cycling is a growing option for adventurous travelers seeking an active way to explore La Palma. The island's varied terrain provides both challenging climbs and rewarding downhill rides, with spectacular views along the way. Mountain biking is popular in forested areas and volcanic landscapes, while road cycling suits those looking for longer, scenic routes along coastal and interior roads. Bicycle rentals are available in towns, and some accommodations cater specifically to cycling tourists with secure storage and repair facilities. Those choosing cycling should be prepared for steep gradients, rapidly changing weather, and occasional traffic on narrow roads.

For transfers within towns or for short sightseeing trips, walking is often the most pleasant option. Santa Cruz de La Palma, with its historic streets, plazas, and harbor, is highly walkable, and exploring on foot allows travelers to appreciate the island's architecture, local markets, and cafes at a relaxed pace. Many coastal villages and scenic viewpoints are accessible by well-marked walking trails, offering an intimate view of La Palma's natural beauty. Comfortable shoes, sun protection, and water are recommended for longer walks, particularly in hilly or sunny areas.

Boat tours and water taxis offer yet another perspective on La Palma's geography. Coastal transport is not only practical for reaching isolated coves and beaches but also provides a chance to experience the island from the sea. Whale and dolphin watching trips, snorkeling excursions, and sightseeing cruises depart regularly from Santa Cruz de La Palma and other ports, combining transportation with adventure. For travelers interested in marine life or unique coastal vistas, these services provide both practicality and memorable experiences.

Airport and ferry transfers can also be organized by many hotels and guesthouses, providing direct service from arrival points to accommodations. These transfers are especially convenient for travelers carrying luggage, families, or anyone preferring a seamless, stress-free start to their visit. Pre-booking is recommended during peak travel periods to ensure availability and punctuality. Staff are generally friendly and knowledgeable, often providing tips about the best routes, scenic stops, and local attractions along the way.

Understanding the basics of La Palma's transport network allows travelers to maximize their exploration while minimizing stress. Whether choosing a rental car for independence, taxis for convenience, buses for economy, or guided transfers for ease and insight, each option provides a way to connect with the island's diverse landscapes, towns, and hidden gems. Proper planning, awareness of schedules, and consideration of terrain and distance are crucial to enjoying a smooth and enjoyable travel experience.

Transfers and transport on La Palma are more than just logistics—they are part of the journey itself. The winding roads, dramatic mountain passes, and coastal drives reveal the island's beauty at every turn, offering glimpses of volcanic formations, lush forests, and ocean views. Each mode of transport presents its own perspective, whether the freedom of driving, the insight of guided tours, or the leisurely approach of public transport. In every case, navigating the island's transport options is an integral step in fully experiencing La Palma's landscapes, culture, and charm.

Chapter 3

First Impressions

The Island's Charm

La Palma's charm is a combination of natural beauty, cultural heritage, and an unhurried pace of life that distinguishes it from many other tourist destinations. Often called "La Isla Bonita," the island lives up to its name in every sense, offering travelers an experience that feels both intimate and awe-inspiring. From the moment you arrive, whether by air or sea, the island radiates a quiet allure: lush green mountains, volcanic landscapes, quaint towns, and the deep blue Atlantic all contribute to a setting that feels almost magical. This charm is not manufactured for tourism; it is intrinsic to the island itself, cultivated over centuries of history, nature, and tradition.

The natural landscapes are central to La Palma's appeal. The island is dominated by volcanic mountains and the enormous Caldera de Taburiente, a crater that stretches for kilometers and forms a dramatic centerpiece of the island. Forests of laurel, pine, and endemic flora cover the slopes, creating misty, almost mystical scenery. Rivers and waterfalls carve through the terrain, adding movement and sound to the serene vistas. The contrast between verdant forests and volcanic black sands along the coast is striking, creating visual diversity that captivates travelers at every turn.

Coastal cliffs, particularly along the western and northern shores, enhance La Palma's charm. These cliffs rise sharply from the Atlantic, often providing unobstructed panoramic views of the ocean that are particularly striking at sunrise and sunset. Small coves, accessible only via hiking trails or boat, add an element of adventure and discovery. Visitors often describe the coastline as a dramatic blend of ruggedness and beauty, a place where every viewpoint offers a new perspective on the island's natural artistry.

Beyond the scenery, La Palma's towns and villages exude a historical charm. Santa Cruz de La Palma, the island's capital, is a living museum of colonial architecture. Narrow cobbled streets, colorful balconies, and historic plazas invite exploration, and the preserved facades of 16th- and 17th-century buildings offer a tangible link to the past. Los Llanos de Aridane, by contrast, presents a livelier urban vibe, with markets, cafes, and cultural events reflecting the contemporary lifestyle of the island's residents. Even the smallest villages, perched on hillsides or tucked into valleys, radiate charm through their simplicity, traditional architecture, and the welcoming spirit of their inhabitants.

The pace of life on La Palma contributes significantly to its allure. Unlike busier tourist destinations, the island encourages a slower rhythm. Days are often spent exploring at one's own pace, hiking scenic trails, enjoying long meals of fresh local cuisine, or simply sitting at a viewpoint to admire the sunset. The lack of crowds in many areas enhances the sense of intimacy and connection with the surroundings. Travelers frequently comment on the sense of tranquility they feel here, a rare combination of nature, culture, and peace that becomes a lasting memory.

Cultural traditions also add depth to the island's charm. Local festivals, music, and artisanal crafts reflect a history that spans both Guanche heritage and Spanish colonial influence. Visitors may encounter religious processions, traditional folk dances, or small village fairs where locals gather to celebrate seasonal events. These cultural touches, often subtle but deeply rooted, enrich the travel experience by offering insight into the lives of the people who call La Palma home. The authenticity of these experiences is a key aspect of the island's appeal.

La Palma's starry skies enhance its charm in a unique way. Designated as a Starlight Reserve, the island is renowned for exceptionally clear night skies, free from light pollution. Observatories and stargazing tours allow travelers to witness the Milky Way, planets, and distant galaxies in vivid detail. This celestial aspect of La Palma is not only scientifically significant but also contributes to the island's magical and almost ethereal atmosphere, making nights as captivating as days.

The local gastronomy also plays a role in the island's attraction. Simple yet flavorful dishes like papas arrugadas with mojo sauces, fresh seafood, tropical fruits, and volcanic wines highlight the connection between the land and the table. Food markets, family-run restaurants, and vineyard visits allow travelers to taste the island in a literal sense, deepening their appreciation for La Palma's natural and cultural richness. Every meal can become a memorable moment, further adding to the island's charm.

Adventure and accessibility coexist harmoniously on La Palma, enhancing its overall appeal. Trails wind through forests, along cliffs, and up volcanic slopes, providing options for both casual walkers and experienced hikers. Beaches, though smaller and often secluded, offer spaces for relaxation and water sports. The combination of exploration, natural beauty, and comfort ensures that every visitor finds something that resonates personally, whether it is a quiet hike, a culinary delight, or simply a moment of reflection at a scenic viewpoint.

Ultimately, La Palma's charm lies in its ability to create meaningful experiences at every turn. The island is not merely a backdrop for sightseeing; it is an active participant in the journey, offering surprises, serenity, and inspiration. Every hike through a laurel forest, every stroll through a historic street, every glance at the night sky reinforces the feeling that La Palma is a place unlike any other. Its natural wonders, vibrant culture, and welcoming people combine to create an island experience that lingers in memory long after the trip ends.

Sights that Impress

La Palma is an island of contrasts and dramatic landscapes, and its sights leave a lasting impression on every visitor. From towering volcanic craters to quaint colonial towns, the island offers a visual feast that combines natural wonders, historic architecture, and cultural landmarks. Exploring La Palma is like turning the pages of a vivid storybook, where every scene is carefully composed to inspire awe, curiosity, and a sense of discovery. For travelers seeking both iconic landmarks and hidden gems, La Palma offers experiences that are unforgettable.

One of the island's most remarkable sights is the Caldera de Taburiente National Park. This massive volcanic crater dominates the center of La Palma, with steep cliffs that rise dramatically from the valley floor. Visitors are drawn to the caldera for its hiking trails, cascading waterfalls, and lush pine forests. From viewpoints such as La Cumbrecita, the panorama of the crater and the surrounding mountains is breathtaking. The interplay of light and shadow across the caldera throughout the day provides endless photographic opportunities, and the crisp mountain air enhances the sense of being in a pristine, unspoiled environment.

Roque de los Muchachos, located near the caldera, is another must-see destination. It is the highest point on La Palma, offering panoramic views of the island and the Atlantic Ocean. The observatories perched on the peak underline La Palma's status as a Starlight Reserve, and the clarity of the skies from this vantage point is extraordinary. Sunrise and sunset are particularly magical here, when clouds may drift below the mountaintop, giving the impression of standing above a sea of mist. Hikers and photographers often describe this experience as both humbling and inspiring.

Coastal sights are equally impressive, particularly the dramatic cliffs and volcanic beaches. The western coast, with its jagged cliffs plunging into the Atlantic, provides some of the most photogenic landscapes on the island. Playa de Nogales and Playa de Puerto Espíndola are examples of black sand beaches framed by cliffs and volcanic formations. Reaching these beaches often involves hiking trails or scenic drives, adding a sense of adventure to the reward of arriving at such striking scenery. The contrast of dark volcanic sand, deep blue water, and lush greenery creates a visual signature that is uniquely La Palma.

Santa Cruz de La Palma itself is a sight worth exploring. The capital's historic streets, adorned with colorful balconies and colonial architecture, reveal centuries of history. Plaza España, with its historic buildings and open-air cafés, is a focal point of city life, while the town's waterfront promenade offers views of the Atlantic and the harbor. Walking through the city, travelers can admire churches, plazas, and traditional houses that reflect a blend of Guanche heritage and Spanish colonial influence. The charm of the streets, combined with cultural landmarks, ensures that the city is as impressive as the island's natural wonders.

Los Llanos de Aridane, the island's largest inland town, provides a complementary experience. Its lively plazas, markets, and cultural centers showcase La Palma's contemporary life and vibrant community. Architecture here combines modern conveniences with traditional styles, giving visitors a sense of continuity and evolution. The town serves as a hub for excursions into nearby valleys, forests, and coastal areas, making it a practical and visually engaging starting point for further exploration.

Scenic viewpoints are scattered throughout La Palma, each offering its own perspective on the island's diversity. Mirador de la Cumbrecita, Mirador de los Andenes, and Mirador de San Bartolo are just a few of the spots where visitors can gaze across volcanic valleys, terraced fields, and distant ocean horizons. These viewpoints are accessible by car or on foot, and many provide hiking trails that lead to even more secluded panoramas. The interplay of light, shadow, and color across La Palma's landscape throughout the day enhances the visual drama, ensuring that every visit yields new impressions.

The island's natural diversity extends to its forests and ravines. Laurel forests, particularly in the north, offer a lush, almost otherworldly atmosphere, with moss-covered trees, mist, and a chorus of bird calls. Barrancos, or ravines, carved by centuries of volcanic activity and rainfall, add depth and texture to the terrain. Hikes through these areas reveal hidden waterfalls, endemic plant species, and quiet pockets of solitude. The combination of dense greenery, geological formations, and natural water features makes these sights deeply memorable.

Religious and cultural landmarks also contribute to La Palma's impressive sights. Churches such as Iglesia de El Salvador in Santa Cruz de La Palma, monasteries, and hermitages often sit atop hills or within town centers, providing both spiritual and architectural interest. These sites reveal the island's historical and cultural layers, showing how the local community has developed over centuries. Visiting these landmarks allows travelers to connect with La

Palma's history and cultural identity in a tangible way.

Finally, the night sky itself is a sight that cannot be missed. As a designated Starlight Reserve, La Palma offers unparalleled opportunities for stargazing. Observatories, dedicated tours, and remote highland locations allow visitors to observe constellations, planets, and distant galaxies with exceptional clarity. For many, the night sky rivals the island's daytime vistas, leaving a profound sense of wonder. The combination of terrestrial beauty and celestial spectacle ensures that La Palma's sights impress long after the journey ends.

La Palma's array of sights—from volcanic landscapes and verdant forests to historic towns and starlit skies—offers travelers a rich and layered experience. Each view, trail, and landmark contributes to a sense of discovery, encouraging exploration and appreciation for the island's unique character. Visitors leave with memories of dramatic cliffs, hidden beaches, panoramic mountain vistas, and charming streets, all of which combine to define the island's enduring and captivating charm.

Settling In

After the excitement of arrival and the first glimpses of La Palma's dramatic landscapes, settling in marks the beginning of a deeper connection with the island. Whether you are staying in a bustling town, a quiet village, or a secluded rural retreat, finding your footing and adapting to the rhythms of La Palma sets the tone for an immersive travel experience. This process is more than just unpacking luggage—it involves orienting yourself to the local environment, understanding practicalities, and beginning to feel at home amid the island's unique blend of nature, culture, and daily life.

Accommodations on La Palma range from boutique hotels and traditional guesthouses to rural cottages and luxury villas. Choosing where to stay often depends on your travel style and priorities. Coastal towns like Santa Cruz de La Palma and Los Llanos de Aridane offer convenience, proximity to restaurants, shops, and cultural attractions, and easy access to main roads for excursions. Rural retreats in the highlands or near the Caldera de Taburiente appeal to travelers seeking tranquility, panoramic views, and immersion in nature. Whichever option you select, settling in involves not only comfort but also a sense of connection to your surroundings.

Orientation is an essential part of settling in. Familiarizing yourself with the local area, nearby grocery stores, pharmacies, restaurants, and transport hubs helps ease any initial travel stress. Maps, guidebooks, or mobile navigation apps can be useful, but La Palma also rewards travelers who explore on foot, discovering hidden alleys, charming plazas, and local markets organically. Taking the time to wander around your immediate surroundings allows for spontaneous encounters with locals, glimpses of everyday life, and a better understanding of the island's rhythms.

Connecting with the local community adds depth to the experience of settling in. La Palma's residents are generally warm, approachable, and proud of their island, often offering helpful advice, directions, or recommendations. Engaging with locals in cafés, markets, or small shops provides not only practical guidance but also insight into traditions, customs, and ways of life that enrich the travel experience. Early interactions help travelers feel more comfortable and confident, making exploration more rewarding and less intimidating.

Practical logistics are part of settling in. Renting a car, setting up mobile connectivity, and understanding public transportation schedules allow for smoother exploration. For those arriving by ferry or plane, initial transfers to accommodations may involve taxis, shuttles, or organized transfers, and familiarizing yourself with these options early on reduces stress. Ensuring essentials like local currency, maps, and hiking or beach gear are ready allows travelers to focus on discovery rather than logistics.

Meals play a significant role in the settling-in process. Sampling local cuisine, visiting neighborhood cafés, or trying fresh produce from markets provides an immediate taste of the island's culture. Papas arrugadas with mojo, fresh fish, tropical fruits, and volcanic wines introduce the palate to La Palma's flavors and establish a connection to the land and sea. Even casual meals can offer insight into local routines, communal habits, and culinary traditions, helping travelers feel integrated into the island environment.

Daily rhythms on La Palma are often slower and more relaxed than in major tourist destinations. Recognizing the island's pace helps visitors adjust expectations, particularly for services that may operate on local schedules rather than strict timetables. Shops may open later in the morning and close for siestas, and markets follow seasonal and weekly patterns. Accepting and adapting to this rhythm allows travelers to enjoy their surroundings fully, embracing the tranquility that makes La Palma so distinctive.

For outdoor enthusiasts, settling in often includes initial explorations of nearby natural features. Even short walks to local viewpoints, beaches, or forested trails help travelers acclimate to the island's terrain, climate, and scenery. These first excursions also allow for practical adjustments, such as testing hiking gear, learning local trail markers, and understanding elevation changes. Starting with manageable distances ensures that visitors build confidence while appreciating the island's beauty without overexertion.

Establishing a daily routine, even temporarily, helps travelers feel grounded. Simple practices like morning walks to a café, visiting the market, or spending time at a favorite viewpoint create a sense of familiarity and comfort. These routines allow travelers to transition from being visitors to becoming participants in the daily life of La Palma, enhancing the overall sense of connection and belonging.

Finally, settling in includes a mindset of openness and curiosity. La Palma rewards those who engage with its people, landscapes, and culture thoughtfully. Taking the time to adjust to local customs, explore surroundings gradually, and observe both natural and social nuances lays the groundwork for a meaningful experience. Once settled, travelers can fully embrace the adventures, sights, and stories that the island offers, ensuring that their visit is not only memorable but also deeply immersive.

By focusing on practicalities, local connections, and initial explorations, settling in transforms the first days on La Palma into a seamless and enriching transition. It allows travelers to move confidently from arrival to adventure, establishing a foundation for deeper appreciation of the island's natural wonders, cultural treasures, and everyday life. In doing so, the journey becomes more than sightseeing—it becomes an experience of living, observing, and connecting with the island at every level.

Chapter 4

Where to Stay

Hotels and Resorts

Finding the right accommodation on La Palma is an essential part of a memorable visit. The island caters to a wide range of travelers, from those seeking luxury and comfort to those preferring cozy, traditional stays immersed in nature. Hotels and resorts provide more than just a place to sleep; they often serve as the starting point for adventures, relaxation, and cultural experiences. Whether located in bustling towns, quiet villages, or tucked into the island's verdant highlands, each property offers a unique perspective on La Palma, allowing travelers to connect with both its landscapes and its lifestyle.

Santa Cruz de La Palma, the island's capital, offers a blend of historic charm and modern amenities in its hotels. Many properties are situated within walking distance of the waterfront, local markets, and colonial-era streets. Staying in this area allows visitors to enjoy early morning strolls along the harbor, sip coffee in quaint cafés, and explore museums and galleries without relying on transportation. Boutique hotels in the city often occupy restored historic buildings, featuring traditional architecture, wooden balconies, and courtyards that create an intimate and authentic atmosphere. These accommodations provide travelers with both comfort and immersion in local culture.

Los Llanos de Aridane, the island's largest urban area, offers more contemporary hotels and resorts. Many of these establishments cater to families and travelers seeking convenience and amenities such as swimming pools, wellness centers, and organized tours. The town's location near fertile valleys, forests, and coastal areas makes it an ideal base for exploring both inland attractions and western beaches. Hotels here often provide guided excursions, car rental services, and information on hiking trails, ensuring that guests have easy access to La Palma's natural and cultural highlights.

For travelers seeking solitude and immersion in nature, rural cottages and eco-lodges scattered throughout the island offer a unique experience. These properties are often situated in quieter highland areas, near volcanic craters, forests, or terraced farmlands. Staying in such locations allows visitors to enjoy panoramic views, starlit skies, and the sounds of nature without the distractions of urban life. Many rural accommodations emphasize sustainability, using local materials, solar energy, and eco-friendly practices, reflecting La Palma's commitment to preserving its environment while providing comfort and authenticity.

Luxury resorts on La Palma cater to those seeking high-end experiences. These properties offer expansive views, swimming pools, gourmet restaurants, and wellness centers, often located in prime locations overlooking the ocean or nestled in scenic valleys. Guests can enjoy services such as spa treatments, guided nature tours, and private excursions, combining relaxation with adventure. These resorts often balance modern design with local architectural elements, ensuring that visitors experience a sense of place while indulging in comfort and luxury.

Accommodation on La Palma is also highly versatile in terms of budget. Small guesthouses, inns, and family-run pensions provide affordable options without compromising charm or quality. These establishments often include personalized service, locally inspired décor, and opportunities to connect with the owners, who can provide insider tips and recommendations. Budget travelers can enjoy comfortable rooms, home-cooked breakfasts, and proximity to key sights, making these options ideal for those who want authenticity and value.

Many hotels and resorts on La Palma offer amenities tailored to active travelers. Properties near hiking trails, volcanic landscapes, and coastal areas provide facilities such as bike storage, guided excursions, and shuttle services to trailheads or beaches. These accommodations serve as strategic bases, allowing travelers to maximize outdoor experiences while returning to comfort and convenience at the end of the day. Families, solo travelers, and adventure enthusiasts alike can find options suited to their needs and preferred level of activity.

Location is a significant factor when selecting accommodations. Coastal hotels provide easy access to beaches and waterfront dining, while highland retreats offer cooler temperatures, hiking opportunities, and panoramic views. Some travelers prefer a central location in towns for convenience, while others choose remote areas for peace and seclusion. Understanding the purpose of the trip, the preferred balance of activity and relaxation, and the desired proximity to key attractions will help guide the choice of lodging.

Booking accommodations in advance is highly recommended, particularly during peak tourist seasons such as summer and winter holidays. Many properties offer direct booking through websites, local tourism offices, or travel agencies. Early reservations ensure availability, access to preferred rooms, and the potential for better rates. Travelers should also consider reviews, amenities, and proximity to planned activities to make the best choice for their individual preferences and itinerary.

Settling into a hotel or resort is more than just a logistical step; it sets the tone for the entire stay. Comfortable accommodations provide a home base from which travelers can explore La Palma's landscapes, culture, and adventures. Whether waking up to ocean vistas, stepping onto a historic balcony, or enjoying the tranquility of a forested retreat, the right lodging enhances every aspect of the journey. It allows visitors to rest, recharge, and immerse themselves fully in the island's natural and cultural offerings.

Ultimately, La Palma's hotels and resorts reflect the island's diversity, combining comfort, charm, and convenience with stunning settings. From historic boutique stays and vibrant town hotels to secluded eco-lodges and luxury resorts, every property contributes to a richer, more immersive travel experience. Choosing the right accommodation ensures that visitors can explore the island with ease, enjoy local culture, and return each day to a space that feels welcoming, restorative, and uniquely La Palma.

Charming Guesthouses

For travelers seeking an intimate and authentic experience on La Palma, charming guesthouses provide the perfect alternative to larger hotels and resorts. These accommodations offer a blend of comfort, personality, and local flavor, often reflecting the island's history, culture, and natural beauty in their design and atmosphere. Staying in a guesthouse allows visitors to feel at home while enjoying personalized service, insider knowledge from hosts, and a slower, more immersive rhythm that is increasingly rare in mainstream tourism.

Guesthouses are scattered across the island, from the bustling streets of Santa Cruz de La Palma to quiet villages perched in the highlands. In the capital, many properties are located in restored colonial buildings, featuring wooden balconies, tiled floors, and cozy courtyards. These accommodations often blend historical charm with modern amenities, allowing guests to experience the architectural beauty of the city while enjoying the comforts of contemporary travel. Walking through the surrounding streets, visitors can quickly reach cafés, small shops, and cultural landmarks, creating a seamless integration of lodging and local life.

In smaller towns and rural areas, guesthouses often emphasize connection with nature. Highland properties provide stunning views of volcanic valleys, forests, and distant ocean horizons. Staying in these guesthouses allows travelers to wake up to the sounds of birds and the gentle sway of trees, offering a sense of peace and solitude. Many of these properties incorporate eco-friendly practices, such as solar power, rainwater collection, and sustainable building materials, reflecting La Palma's commitment to preserving its unique environment. These guesthouses create a sense of harmony between comfort, style, and ecological responsibility.

Hosts play a significant role in defining the charm of guesthouses. Family-run establishments often provide personalized recommendations for hiking trails, beaches, local festivals, and restaurants. Guests benefit from the insider knowledge of someone who knows the island intimately, gaining access to hidden spots that are off the usual tourist path. This level of personal attention creates a welcoming atmosphere, making travelers feel valued and connected to the community. Many hosts also offer cultural insights, stories about the region's history, and tips on navigating La Palma's winding roads and trails.

The interior design of guesthouses often reflects local traditions and craftsmanship. Handcrafted furniture, decorative tiles, traditional fabrics, and local artwork are common, giving each room a unique personality. Courtyards, terraces, and gardens are frequently part of the property, providing inviting spaces to relax, enjoy breakfast, or simply take in the surrounding scenery. These thoughtful details transform a guesthouse stay into more than just a night's lodging—they create an experience that engages the senses and deepens the connection to La Palma.

Meals in guesthouses often enhance the charm of the stay. Many offer breakfast made from locally sourced ingredients, including fresh bread, tropical fruits, cheeses, and pastries. Some properties even serve homemade jams, local honey, or traditional

Canarian dishes, allowing travelers to begin each day with an authentic taste of the island. Dining at a guesthouse can also foster interactions with other guests, creating opportunities to share experiences, travel tips, and stories from different parts of the world. This social aspect adds another layer of enjoyment to the lodging experience.

Guesthouses also cater to diverse types of travelers. Couples often seek romantic settings with private terraces or scenic views, while solo travelers may enjoy the sociable, welcoming atmosphere. Families can benefit from accommodations that offer communal spaces and kitchen facilities, allowing for flexible meal options and convenience. Even adventurers and hikers appreciate guesthouses located near trails, volcanic parks, or coastal paths, as they provide a comfortable base after long days of exploration. The adaptability of these accommodations makes them appealing to a broad spectrum of visitors.

Booking a guesthouse requires consideration of both location and style. Central properties are ideal for exploring towns, markets, and cultural attractions on foot, while rural or highland guesthouses provide direct access to natural landscapes, hiking trails, and starry night skies. Reading reviews, checking amenities, and understanding the host's offerings ensures that guests select a property that aligns with their travel priorities, whether that means comfort, tranquility, accessibility, or local immersion.

Many guesthouses emphasize sustainable and responsible tourism. From organic gardens and solar energy to careful waste management and promotion of local products, these accommodations integrate environmental consciousness into the travel experience. Choosing a guesthouse that prioritizes sustainability allows travelers to reduce their ecological footprint while supporting local communities. This approach aligns with La Palma's overall commitment to preserving its natural landscapes, making a guesthouse stay both responsible and enriching.

Ultimately, charming guesthouses provide a more personal, authentic, and memorable way to experience La Palma. They combine comfort with character, service with intimacy, and location with immersion, allowing travelers to connect deeply with the island's culture, landscape, and people. For those who value meaningful experiences over standard accommodations, guesthouses offer a unique perspective on La Palma, creating a home away from home while enhancing every moment of the journey.

Unique Stays

La Palma offers travelers a variety of unique stays that go beyond traditional hotels and guesthouses, adding an element of adventure, creativity, and individuality to their visit. These accommodations cater to those seeking experiences that reflect the island's natural beauty, cultural heritage, or distinctive lifestyle. From eco-lodges nestled in volcanic landscapes to restored fincas, treehouses, and even boutique cave dwellings, La Palma's unique stays provide an immersive perspective that transforms lodging into an integral part of the journey.

Eco-lodges and sustainable retreats are among the most appealing options for environmentally conscious travelers. Located in the highlands, forests, or volcanic areas, these properties are designed to blend harmoniously with their surroundings. They often feature solar-powered energy, rainwater collection systems, and locally sourced building materials. Staying in an eco-lodge allows visitors to experience the island's natural beauty up close, with panoramic views of valleys, craters, and the Atlantic Ocean. Many also offer guided nature tours, hiking excursions, and wellness activities such as yoga, creating a holistic experience that nurtures both body and mind.

Rural fincas, or traditional Canarian farmhouses, offer another type of unique stay. These restored properties often retain original architectural features, including wooden beams, stone walls, and terracotta tiles, while providing modern comforts. Guests can enjoy private terraces, gardens, and the tranquility of the countryside, far from the crowds of the main towns. Many fincas are situated near vineyards, orchards, or hiking trails, allowing travelers to immerse themselves in La Palma's agricultural traditions and natural landscapes. Some even provide opportunities to participate in seasonal farming activities, offering a hands-on experience that deepens cultural appreciation.

For adventurous travelers, treehouses, cabins, and remote lodges provide a sense of escape and novelty. These accommodations are often perched in forests, on cliff edges, or near secluded beaches, creating a feeling of being fully enveloped by nature. Waking up to the sounds of birds, ocean waves, or rustling leaves, guests experience an intimate connection with the island's environment. Many such stays incorporate eco-friendly practices, outdoor living spaces, and minimalistic design, emphasizing a return to simplicity and a focus on the sensory beauty of the surroundings.

La Palma also has a selection of boutique and artistic accommodations that cater to travelers seeking creativity and individuality. Small hotels or studios often display local artwork, feature themed rooms, or use design elements inspired by the island's volcanic geology, forests, or ocean vistas. These spaces offer more than just a place to sleep—they provide an aesthetic experience that stimulates the imagination and reflects La Palma's cultural richness. Guests often find that these accommodations inspire relaxation, reflection, and a deeper engagement with the local atmosphere.

Some unique stays are built into or near geological formations, providing an unparalleled connection to La Palma's volcanic heritage. Cave homes, lava rock lodges, or cliffside retreats allow guests to experience the raw power and beauty of the island's natural history. These accommodations often include terraces or observation points, offering unobstructed views of the surrounding landscapes, distant ocean horizons, or starlit skies at night. Staying in such a location transforms the overnight experience into a dialogue with the island's geological past, making each night memorable and extraordinary.

Another compelling feature of unique stays on La Palma is the sense of privacy and exclusivity they provide. Many are located away from busy streets and tourist hubs, offering peaceful retreats where guests can disconnect from daily life and fully immerse themselves in the island's rhythms. Whether it is enjoying a private pool overlooking the Atlantic, a secluded garden surrounded by pine forests, or a starry night on a remote terrace, these accommodations allow for reflection, rejuvenation, and a personal encounter with La Palma's natural and cultural wealth.

Amenities in unique stays vary widely but often emphasize authenticity and comfort rather than luxury alone. Outdoor seating areas, fully equipped kitchens, or cozy fireplaces enhance the experience, while guided tours, wellness programs, and curated local experiences allow guests to engage with the island beyond their accommodation. Many properties collaborate with local producers, artists, and guides, further connecting visitors with the culture and environment of La Palma.

Booking these distinctive accommodations requires research and planning, as many properties are smaller, privately managed, and highly seasonal. Direct booking through websites, tourism platforms, or recommendations from travel guides ensures availability and provides insight into what makes each property special. Reading reviews, examining amenities, and considering location relative to planned activities are essential steps to ensure the chosen stay aligns with both practical needs and personal preferences.

Ultimately, La Palma's unique stays transform lodging into an experience that complements the island's natural beauty, cultural richness, and adventurous spirit. From eco-lodges and rural fincas to treehouses, artistic retreats, and geological hideaways, these accommodations offer more than comfort—they create lasting memories, provide immersive experiences, and allow travelers to engage deeply with La Palma's essence. For those seeking something beyond the ordinary, these unique stays define the island as a place where every moment, including where you rest, becomes part of the adventure.

Chapter 5

Adventures

Hiking Trails and Volcano Tours

La Palma is often referred to as the "Isla Verde" or Green Island, and for good reason. Its lush landscapes, rugged mountains, volcanic formations, and verdant forests make it a paradise for hikers, nature enthusiasts, and adventure seekers. Exploring the island on foot is one of the most immersive ways to experience its diverse scenery, allowing travelers to witness the dramatic contrasts between volcanic landscapes, dense laurel forests, and the deep blue Atlantic Ocean. Hiking trails and volcano tours are central to understanding La Palma's unique geology, ecology, and natural charm.

The Caldera de Taburiente National Park is the crown jewel of La Palma's hiking trails. This enormous volcanic crater, surrounded by towering cliffs, offers a range of trails suited to different levels of experience. The descent into the caldera, through lush pine forests and past sparkling streams, is both physically rewarding and visually stunning. Trails vary from short walks to multi-day treks, with viewpoints such as Mirador de La Cumbrecita providing panoramic vistas of the crater floor, waterfalls, and surrounding mountains. Hiking here allows visitors to feel the scale of the island's volcanic forces and appreciate the delicate balance of flora and fauna within the caldera.

Volcano tours are another highlight of La Palma's outdoor adventures. The island's volcanic origins are visible almost everywhere, from black sand beaches to lava fields and cinder cones. Guided tours offer a safe and informative way to explore these areas, often combining hiking with geological insights. Walking across cooled lava flows, observing the patterns of past eruptions, and understanding the formation of volcanic landscapes give travelers a deep appreciation for the island's dynamic history. Volcano tours often include visits to active viewpoints, allowing hikers to see volcanic features up close while learning about their impact on the island's development and ecosystems.

One of the most popular volcanic routes is the ascent of the San Antonio and Teneguía volcanoes in the southern part of the island. The Teneguía volcano, which last erupted in 1971, provides a surreal landscape of black lava fields and ash-covered terrain. The trails here are relatively accessible, making them suitable for most visitors, and the views of the surrounding ocean and coastline enhance the dramatic experience. San Antonio, with its crater and interpretive signs, complements the Teneguía route, offering insight into volcanic activity, flora colonization, and conservation efforts.

For those seeking forested trails, the laurel forests in the northern and central highlands of La Palma are breathtaking. Areas such as Los Tilos, a UNESCO Biosphere Reserve, provide winding paths through dense greenery, moss-covered trees, and streams that feed into hidden waterfalls. Hiking in these forests offers not only exercise and scenic views but also encounters with endemic bird species and plant life unique to the island. The combination of mist, filtered sunlight, and vibrant flora creates an almost ethereal atmosphere, making these treks particularly memorable.

The island also offers longer, multi-day hiking opportunities. The Ruta de los Volcanes, a trail stretching along the island's volcanic ridge from the south to the north, is renowned for its dramatic landscapes and varying terrain. Hikers traverse lava fields, volcanic cones, and high-altitude paths, with opportunities to pause at small villages for rest and local cuisine. This trek offers some of the most spectacular viewpoints on La Palma, including vistas of the ocean, cliffs, and the island's interior valleys. Multi-day hikes like this require preparation, proper gear, and sometimes guidance from local experts, but they reward travelers with an unparalleled sense of immersion and accomplishment.

Shorter, accessible trails also provide a rich hiking experience for casual walkers. Coastal walks, such as those near the villages of Puerto Naos and Tazacorte, allow visitors to enjoy ocean views, palm groves, and volcanic beaches without strenuous effort. Trails in the highlands, such as Mirador de los Andenes or viewpoints around Roque de los Muchachos, provide spectacular panoramas with less physical exertion. These shorter hikes are perfect for travelers who want to experience La Palma's natural beauty in a single morning or afternoon, combining convenience with visual reward.

Guided hikes and volcano tours are available throughout the island, providing educational insights into geology, ecology, and local history.

Knowledgeable guides explain the formation of volcanic landscapes, the regeneration of flora after eruptions, and the cultural significance of certain areas. Many tours also include safety equipment, maps, and support for navigating difficult terrain, making them suitable for families, solo travelers, and groups. These guided experiences often uncover hidden spots and secret trails that are otherwise difficult to find, enhancing the sense of discovery.

Safety and preparation are important considerations for hiking in La Palma. Trails can be steep, rocky, and exposed to the elements, so sturdy footwear, sun protection, sufficient water, and layered clothing are essential. Weather conditions can change rapidly, particularly at higher elevations, so hikers should always check forecasts and allow extra time for their excursions. Being prepared ensures that the focus remains on enjoying the landscapes, wildlife, and the unique volcanic scenery rather than dealing with preventable challenges.

Hiking and volcano tours in La Palma are more than physical activities—they are immersive journeys that connect travelers to the island's geology, ecology, and spirit. Each trail offers a combination of adventure, education, and visual delight, allowing visitors to appreciate both the power and the beauty of the island. From dramatic volcanic craters and black sand beaches to lush forests and panoramic ridges, every step reveals new perspectives, making La Palma a destination where the journey itself is as memorable as the destinations.

Water Sports and Beaches

La Palma may be famed for its mountains and volcanic landscapes, but its coastline offers an equally compelling array of experiences. The island's beaches and surrounding waters are diverse, ranging from black volcanic sand stretches to hidden coves and rocky shorelines. These coastal areas not only provide a place to relax and soak in the sun but also serve as playgrounds for water sports enthusiasts, adventure seekers, and nature lovers. Engaging with the island's marine environment allows travelers to experience La Palma from a new perspective, combining physical activity, scenic beauty, and the simple pleasure of being close to the Atlantic Ocean.

Beaches on La Palma are distinctive due to the island's volcanic origins. Unlike the golden sands of some other Canary Islands, many of La Palma's beaches feature dramatic black sand and pebbles, creating striking contrasts against the turquoise waters. Playa de Nogales, often considered one of the island's most scenic beaches, is framed by cliffs and lush greenery. Its powerful waves attract surfers and bodyboarders, while the surrounding cliffs provide panoramic views for those who prefer to relax onshore. The dramatic volcanic backdrop creates a setting that feels both wild and intimate, ideal for photography and quiet reflection.

Playa de Puerto Espíndola, in the northern part of the island, offers a more secluded atmosphere. Accessible via hiking trails or narrow coastal roads, this beach is perfect for travelers seeking privacy and connection with nature. The black sand, combined with gently rolling waves, creates a serene environment for sunbathing, swimming, or simply enjoying the rhythmic sounds of the ocean. Its remoteness contributes to a sense of discovery, as reaching it feels like uncovering a hidden gem.

Swimming and snorkeling are popular activities along La Palma's coasts. Clear waters near sheltered bays and coves provide excellent visibility for observing marine life, including colorful fish, sea urchins, and occasionally octopuses. The northern and western shores have rocky formations and natural pools where snorkeling enthusiasts can explore safely. Some areas, such as Charco Azul in San Andrés y Sauces, feature natural tidal pools formed by volcanic rock, offering calm waters ideal for families and casual swimmers. These natural pools combine adventure and safety, allowing visitors to enjoy marine encounters in a protected environment.

For those seeking active water sports, La Palma provides opportunities for surfing, windsurfing, kayaking, and paddleboarding. The island's exposure to Atlantic winds and waves creates favorable conditions for both beginners and experienced surfers, with surf schools and equipment rentals available in key coastal towns. Kayaking and paddleboarding are popular along calm bays and near coastal cliffs, offering a unique vantage point from which to view the island's volcanic formations, seabirds, and hidden beaches. Guided tours often combine exercise with ecological education, highlighting local marine life and conservation efforts.

Scuba diving is another way to explore La Palma's underwater world. The island's volcanic reefs and clear waters provide excellent conditions for diving, with numerous dive centers offering lessons and excursions for all skill levels. Divers can encounter lava formations, caves, and a rich array of marine species, from vibrant fish to larger pelagic creatures. Night dives offer a different perspective, revealing nocturnal behaviors of marine life and adding an element of adventure. Scuba enthusiasts consistently rank La Palma as one of the Canary Islands' most fascinating diving destinations due to its diverse underwater landscapes.

Safety and environmental awareness are essential when enjoying La Palma's beaches and water sports. Volcanic shores can have strong currents, sudden drop-offs, and slippery rocks, so caution is always advised. Many beaches display warning signs for swimming conditions, and local lifeguards provide additional guidance during peak seasons. Respecting marine habitats, avoiding litter, and following local regulations ensure that the island's coastal beauty is preserved for future visitors. Conscious participation allows travelers to enjoy the environment responsibly while minimizing impact.

Even for those who prefer relaxation to activity, La Palma's beaches offer plenty of charm. Sunbathing on black sand, picnicking on rocky terraces, or enjoying a quiet sunset by the water allows visitors to absorb the island's atmosphere at a leisurely pace. Small beachfront cafés and kiosks provide refreshments, local snacks, and opportunities to mingle with residents and fellow travelers. The combination of natural beauty and casual coastal culture creates an inviting setting for unwinding after a day of hiking, sightseeing, or adventure.

La Palma's coastline also provides opportunities for exploration beyond the beaches themselves. Scenic walking paths along cliffs, coastal viewpoints, and short hikes to hidden coves reveal secret spots that many travelers miss. These excursions offer a mix of visual reward and gentle physical activity, allowing visitors to engage with the environment in diverse ways. Photographers, nature lovers, and casual explorers alike will find that every turn along the coast presents a new perspective on the island's rugged beauty.

Ultimately, the combination of water sports and beaches enhances La Palma's appeal as a versatile travel destination. The island balances adventure, relaxation, and natural wonder, allowing travelers to engage with the ocean in multiple ways—from adrenaline-fueled surfing to quiet moments in a secluded cove. La Palma's coasts, with their volcanic sands, clear waters, and dramatic cliffs, create lasting impressions, adding another layer to the island's charm and ensuring that the seaside experience is as memorable as its mountains, forests, and villages.

Exploring the Natural Wonders

La Palma is often celebrated as one of the most beautiful and ecologically diverse islands in the Canary Islands, and exploring its natural wonders is central to understanding its allure. From volcanic craters and lush forests to rugged cliffs and sparkling waterfalls, the island offers an extraordinary variety of landscapes that seem to exist in miniature yet encompass the drama of the natural world. Every corner of La Palma presents an opportunity to witness geological processes, endemic flora and fauna, and breathtaking vistas, making it a paradise for nature lovers, adventurers, and those seeking to reconnect with the environment.

The Caldera de Taburiente National Park is the most iconic of La Palma's natural wonders. This massive volcanic crater, with its steep cliffs and verdant valleys, is a living laboratory of geological and ecological processes. Hiking trails crisscross the park, allowing visitors to explore hidden waterfalls, pine forests, and streams that have carved their way through the rock over millennia. The caldera's sheer size and dramatic topography create a sense of grandeur that is rare even among volcanic landscapes, offering breathtaking panoramas at every turn. Visitors often remark on the feeling of being enveloped by nature, where every sight, sound, and scent contributes to a profound sense of place.

Volcanic landscapes extend across the island, from the southern Teneguía volcano to smaller cones and lava fields scattered along the coast. These areas showcase the raw power of natural forces and provide opportunities for exploration and learning. Walking over cooled lava flows, observing the patterns of past eruptions, and understanding the formation of volcanic craters offer insights into the dynamic processes that shaped La Palma. Guided tours and interpretive trails help travelers comprehend the island's volcanic history while navigating these rugged terrains safely, making the experience both educational and awe-inspiring.

La Palma's forests are another highlight of its natural wonders. The laurel forests, particularly in the northern and central highlands, are dense, mossy, and almost mystical. These UNESCO-protected areas provide a cool, shaded retreat from the sun, with trails that wind through ancient trees and along bubbling streams. The rich biodiversity includes endemic birds, unique plant species, and occasional sightings of reptiles or small mammals. Walking through these forests feels like stepping back in time, as the ecosystem has remained largely unchanged for centuries. The combination of mist, filtered sunlight, and dense vegetation creates an immersive, almost magical atmosphere that stays with visitors long after they leave.

Water features add another layer of wonder to La Palma's landscapes. Natural pools, waterfalls, and coastal coves provide both aesthetic beauty and recreational opportunities. The Charco Azul in San Andrés y Sauces is a prime example, where volcanic rock formations have created serene swimming areas with crystal-clear waters. Hidden waterfalls in valleys such as the Barranco de las Angustias or Los Tilos are often discovered along hiking routes, rewarding those willing to explore with refreshing sights and sounds. The interplay of water and volcanic terrain exemplifies the island's dynamic natural environment.

Coastal cliffs and viewpoints further define La Palma's natural identity. The western and northern coasts feature jagged cliffs plunging into the Atlantic, creating dramatic vistas that change with the light and weather. Miradors, or scenic viewpoints, are strategically located to offer panoramic perspectives of the coastline, terraced fields, and distant ocean horizons. From these vantage points, visitors can witness the island's contrasting landscapes—from lush valleys and pine-covered slopes to barren volcanic ridges—demonstrating the diversity and complexity of La Palma's terrain.

Flora and fauna are integral to the island's natural wonders. Endemic species of plants, such as the Canary Island pine and various laurel trees, thrive in

La Palma's microclimates. Birdwatchers can spot the laurel pigeon, the Canary Island chiffchaff, and other unique species that inhabit the island's forests and cliffs. The preservation of these ecosystems is a testament to the island's environmental awareness and offers travelers a rare opportunity to experience biodiversity in a relatively undisturbed setting. Observing these species in their natural habitats deepens appreciation for the delicate balance of life on La Palma.

For those seeking adventure in nature, La Palma provides ample opportunities beyond hiking and sightseeing. Caving, canyoning, and guided ecological tours allow visitors to explore hidden areas, underground lava tubes, and remote valleys. Adventure activities often combine physical challenge with educational insights, providing a richer understanding of the island's natural processes. These experiences highlight both the beauty and resilience of La Palma's landscapes while satisfying the curiosity of travelers eager to engage with the environment actively.

La Palma's stargazing opportunities are also part of its natural allure. The island is a designated Starlight Reserve, meaning its skies are exceptionally clear and protected from light pollution. Observatories such as those at Roque de los Muchachos allow visitors to gaze at stars, planets, and galaxies with extraordinary clarity. Experiencing the night sky in this context—after a day of exploring craters, forests, and cliffs—adds a celestial dimension to the island's natural wonders. The sense of scale and connection to the universe is a profound complement to the terrestrial landscapes below.

Engaging with La Palma's natural wonders is not just a sightseeing activity—it is an invitation to experience the island fully. Each hike, beach visit, forest walk, or volcanic exploration offers a sensory connection to the environment. Travelers leave with memories of dramatic cliffs, misty forests, shimmering waterfalls, and starlit skies, gaining a deeper appreciation for the island's unique ecosystems. By immersing themselves in these natural experiences, visitors not only enjoy unforgettable adventures but also develop an awareness of the island's conservation efforts, making their journey both enriching and responsible.

Chapter 6

Local Flavors

Must-Try Dishes

No visit to La Palma is complete without exploring its rich culinary landscape, where traditional Canarian flavors meet fresh, locally sourced ingredients. The island's cuisine reflects its volcanic soils, fertile valleys, and coastal resources, offering a variety of dishes that are hearty, flavorful, and deeply connected to local culture. From street food and casual eateries to family-run restaurants and high-end dining, La Palma presents a culinary journey that engages the senses and provides insight into the island's history, traditions, and daily life.

One of the most iconic dishes on La Palma is papas arrugadas, or wrinkled potatoes. These small, salty potatoes are boiled in heavily salted water, often until the skins develop a characteristic wrinkled texture. They are typically served with mojo sauces—mojo rojo, a red pepper and garlic sauce, and mojo verde, made from cilantro, parsley, and garlic. The combination of earthy potatoes with vibrant, tangy sauces is simple yet incredibly satisfying, offering a perfect introduction to the island's flavors. Many restaurants serve papas arrugadas as a side dish, but they can also be enjoyed as a snack at markets or street stands.

Fresh seafood is a cornerstone of La Palma's culinary identity. The island's surrounding Atlantic waters provide an abundance of fish, octopus, squid, and shellfish. Dishes such as sancocho, a salted fish stew often accompanied by sweet potatoes and mojo, highlight the skillful balance of local ingredients. Grilled fish, marinated in olive oil, garlic, and local herbs, is another favorite, frequently served in seaside restaurants with stunning ocean views. Seafood not only offers an authentic taste of the island but also underscores the connection between La Palma's coastal communities and their maritime traditions.

Cheese is another essential component of La Palma's gastronomy. The island produces a variety of artisanal cheeses, often made from goat or cow's milk. Queso de cabra, a soft or semi-hard goat cheese, is frequently served with mojo, as part of tapas, or grilled as a warm appetizer. Aged cheeses, sometimes rubbed with paprika or coated in volcanic ash, offer deeper, more robust flavors. Sampling these cheeses provides insight into traditional agricultural practices and the importance of dairy production in the island's economy and culture.

La Palma is also known for its sweet treats and desserts. Bienmesabe, a traditional almond-based dessert made with honey and egg yolks, is often served with ice cream or as a cake filling. Truchas de batata, sweet pastries filled with sweet potato, sugar, and cinnamon, are especially popular during local festivals and holidays. These desserts reflect the island's blend of Spanish, Moorish, and indigenous culinary influences, showcasing how centuries of history have shaped La Palma's unique flavors. Local bakeries and cafés are ideal places to sample these sweets while enjoying the warm, inviting atmosphere of a small town or village.

Tropical fruits thrive in La Palma's fertile climate, adding freshness and vibrancy to meals. Bananas, avocados, papayas, and mangoes are widely available and often feature in both savory and sweet dishes. Fresh fruit is also used in juices, smoothies, and desserts, providing a refreshing complement to richer dishes. Seasonal fruits reflect the island's microclimates, with different regions producing varying crops, which encourages visitors to explore local markets and sample produce directly from growers.

La Palma's tapas culture allows travelers to taste a variety of dishes in one meal, offering a microcosm of the island's culinary diversity. Small plates of grilled vegetables, cheeses, seafood, and traditional stews provide a sampling of flavors, textures, and cooking techniques. Tapas bars often foster a lively social environment, encouraging conversation, shared experiences, and discovery of new flavors. Enjoying tapas is not just about food—it is a cultural experience, offering insight into how locals gather, celebrate, and savor their cuisine.

Local wines are another highlight of La Palma's gastronomic offerings. Vineyards in the southern valleys produce crisp whites, rich reds, and unique volcanic varietals that pair beautifully with island dishes. Wine tours and tastings provide travelers with an understanding of traditional viticulture, the influence of volcanic soil on flavor, and the pride that winemakers take in their craft. Sampling La Palma's wines enhances meals and adds a layer of sensory enjoyment, connecting visitors with the island's agricultural heritage and culinary creativity.

Dining on La Palma often emphasizes fresh, seasonal, and local ingredients. Many restaurants source produce, meat, and seafood from nearby farms and fisheries, supporting sustainability and ensuring quality. This focus on locality enhances the flavors of dishes while connecting travelers with the island's community and traditions. Visitors are encouraged to ask about ingredients, preparation methods, and seasonal specialties to fully appreciate the care and craftsmanship behind each meal.

Ultimately, La Palma's must-try dishes reflect the island's identity, history, and environment. From the simplicity of papas arrugadas with mojo to the rich flavors of seafood stews, artisanal cheeses, tropical fruits, and traditional desserts, every bite tells a story. Sampling these dishes provides more than nourishment—it offers a gateway to understanding the island's culture, connecting travelers to its people, landscapes, and heritage. Culinary exploration becomes an essential part of the La Palma experience, ensuring that every meal contributes to lasting memories of this extraordinary island.

Cafes and Markets

Immersing yourself in La Palma's culture is not complete without experiencing its vibrant cafes and bustling markets. These spaces are more than just places to eat or shop—they are hubs of social interaction, centers of local commerce, and windows into the island's traditions and daily life. From quaint street-side coffee shops to lively farmers' markets brimming with fresh produce and artisan crafts, cafes and markets provide an authentic way to engage with the people, flavors, and atmosphere of La Palma.

Cafes on La Palma are varied, ranging from contemporary coffee houses to traditional Spanish cafés with historic charm. Many are tucked along cobblestone streets in towns such as Santa Cruz de La Palma or Los Llanos de Aridane, often with outdoor seating that allows visitors to watch the ebb and flow of daily life. Cafes serve more than just coffee—they offer pastries, fresh juices, and local specialties such as almond cakes, churros, or bienmesabe. Sitting at a café provides an opportunity to slow down, observe the surroundings, and absorb the rhythm of island life, whether in the early morning bustle or the relaxed afternoon lull.

Coffee culture on La Palma is influenced by the broader Spanish tradition but also incorporates local twists. Cafes often serve espresso, cortado, or café con leche, paired with freshly baked goods from nearby bakeries. Specialty coffee shops have emerged in recent years, offering artisan brews, alternative milk options, and even workshops on brewing techniques. Whether you prefer a quick pick-me-up before a hike or a leisurely coffee with friends, the island's cafes provide an inviting setting to savor both beverages and ambiance.

Markets on La Palma are equally essential to understanding local culture. Weekly farmers' markets, particularly in towns like Los Llanos, Santa Cruz, and El Paso, are abundant with fresh produce, homemade cheeses, honey, tropical fruits, and baked goods. These markets are a feast for the senses: vivid colors of fruits and vegetables, the aromas of freshly baked bread and pastries, and the lively chatter of locals bargaining and sharing news. Visiting a market allows travelers to experience the island's agricultural diversity, sample seasonal delicacies, and interact directly with producers who are proud to share their craft.

Artisan crafts are another highlight of La Palma's markets. Stalls frequently feature handmade ceramics, woven baskets, embroidered textiles, wooden carvings, and jewelry crafted by local artisans. Many of these crafts are inspired by the island's natural landscapes, incorporating motifs from volcanic formations, ocean waves, or endemic flora. Purchasing items from these markets not only supports the local economy but also allows travelers to take home tangible pieces of La Palma's culture and creativity. Each item tells a story, reflecting both tradition and the personal expression of the artisan.

In addition to traditional markets, La Palma hosts specialized craft fairs and seasonal events, where visitors can observe live demonstrations of pottery, weaving, or woodworking. These experiences provide a deeper understanding of the techniques, patience, and artistry involved in creating each piece. Travelers often find that these events foster connection, curiosity, and appreciation for the island's rich cultural heritage, making them more than just shopping excursions—they are educational and inspiring experiences.

Cafes and markets also serve as social hubs where locals gather, share stories, and engage in community life. Observing this interaction provides travelers with insight into the island's lifestyle, values, and traditions. Striking up a conversation with a shopkeeper or fellow market-goer often leads to recommendations for hidden beaches, scenic viewpoints, or family-run eateries that might not appear in guidebooks. This human connection adds depth to the travel experience, making each visit to a café or market feel personal and memorable.

For food enthusiasts, La Palma's markets offer an opportunity to try seasonal ingredients in their freshest form. Tropical fruits like papayas, bananas, and mangoes, as well as vegetables unique to the Canary Islands, can be sampled on site or purchased to incorporate into meals. Many markets also feature local honey, jams, olive oil, and spices, providing both flavor and insight into the island's culinary practices. Cooking classes or tastings are sometimes available, further enhancing the interactive experience and connecting visitors with the flavors of La Palma.

Timing your visits to cafes and markets can enhance the experience. Early mornings are ideal for observing the bustle of vendors setting up, selecting the freshest produce, and interacting with regular customers. Afternoons provide a more relaxed pace, ideal for enjoying a leisurely coffee, snack, or light meal while people-watching. Seasonal festivals, holidays, and weekend markets add variety and excitement, offering special products, entertainment, and cultural performances. By planning around these rhythms, travelers can enjoy a dynamic and engaging exploration of the island's social and culinary life.

Ultimately, La Palma's cafes and markets are essential portals into the island's character. They combine flavors, smells, sights, and sounds to create a rich tapestry of local life. Whether sipping coffee in a sunlit plaza, exploring a bustling farmers' market, or admiring handmade crafts, visitors gain insight into the traditions, tastes, and community spirit that define the island. These experiences enrich the travel journey, providing connections, memories, and sensory delights that linger long after leaving La Palma.

Sweet Treats

La Palma's culinary landscape would be incomplete without a closer look at its sweet treats, which offer both indulgence and a taste of the island's rich history. From traditional pastries to modern desserts, La Palma's sweets are characterized by their use of local ingredients, creative combinations, and distinctive Canarian flair. Sampling these confections is not merely a culinary activity—it is an immersion into the island's culture, agricultural heritage, and festive traditions. Each sweet tells a story, connecting visitors to the flavors, textures, and rituals that have been cherished by generations of islanders.

One of the most beloved desserts on La Palma is bienmesabe, a creamy almond-based treat often served as a dessert topping or a filling for pastries. Made from ground almonds, sugar, honey, and egg yolks, bienmesabe has a rich, slightly sweet flavor and a smooth, velvety texture. This dessert has its roots in both Spanish and Moorish culinary traditions, reflecting centuries of cultural exchange in the Canary Islands. Local bakeries and cafés often serve bienmesabe alongside ice cream, cakes, or simply by the spoonful, allowing visitors to savor the essence of traditional island flavors.

Another iconic sweet is truchas de batata, a pastry filled with sweet potato, sugar, cinnamon, and sometimes almonds. These pastries are particularly popular during holidays and festivals, but they can also be found year-round in local bakeries. The combination of soft, sweet filling and flaky, lightly browned pastry creates a harmonious contrast that appeals to both the eyes and the palate. Each bite encapsulates La Palma's dedication to simple, high-quality ingredients and careful craftsmanship, providing a comforting, authentic taste of the island.

Tropical fruits play an important role in La Palma's sweet offerings. Bananas, mangoes, papayas, and passion fruits are incorporated into tarts, cakes, and puddings, often paired with locally produced honey or cream. Seasonal fruit preserves, jams, and compotes are frequently used as toppings or fillings, highlighting the freshness and variety of the island's produce. Sampling these fruit-based sweets allows visitors to appreciate the diversity of flavors that flourish in La Palma's fertile soils and subtropical climate.

Local chocolate and confectionery also have a strong presence on the island. Artisanal chocolatiers create handmade chocolates infused with tropical fruits, spices, or Canarian nuts, offering unique and memorable flavors. Some chocolate shops combine traditional techniques with modern creativity, producing treats that are both visually appealing and richly flavored. These sweet delicacies make perfect souvenirs or gifts, providing a tangible taste of La Palma to bring home.

Pastry shops and bakeries are scattered throughout the towns and villages, offering a range of traditional and innovative sweets. Morning visits often reveal freshly baked goods, while afternoon stops provide a chance to sample desserts with coffee or tea. Many bakeries also produce seasonal specialties tied to holidays, religious celebrations, or local festivals, ensuring that every visit has a unique culinary surprise. Engaging with these establishments provides not only delicious treats but also an understanding of the rhythms and traditions of daily life on the island.

Canarian desserts often feature simple ingredients prepared with skill and care. Almonds, honey, sweet potatoes, bananas, and local cheeses are staples in many recipes, reflecting both the island's agricultural heritage and its culinary ingenuity. By highlighting the natural flavors of these ingredients, La Palma's sweet treats remain authentic, balanced, and deeply satisfying. Visitors quickly notice that each dessert carries the essence of the land, its people, and their longstanding culinary traditions.

Festivals and local celebrations often showcase a wide array of sweets, emphasizing the role of desserts in cultural and religious life. During events such as patron saint festivals or Christmas celebrations, special pastries, candies, and confections are prepared and shared among families and neighbors. Participating in these occasions allows travelers to experience sweets in their social and ceremonial context, adding a deeper layer of meaning to each bite. These moments highlight the communal and celebratory aspects of La Palma's culinary culture.

For travelers with a penchant for indulgence, pairing sweet treats with local beverages enhances the experience. A slice of almond cake or a portion of truchas de batata accompanied by a glass of locally produced wine, coffee, or herbal tea provides a sensory journey through taste, aroma, and texture. Many cafés offer curated dessert menus with suggested pairings, allowing visitors to enjoy a well-rounded and harmonious experience that reflects the care and tradition behind each creation.

Ultimately, La Palma's sweet treats are more than mere desserts—they are edible stories of culture, history, and craftsmanship. Each pastry, cake, or confection offers a connection to the island's people, landscape, and traditions. Sampling these delights allows travelers to engage with La Palma in a deeply sensory and memorable way, making each sweet indulgence an essential part of the island experience. From traditional classics to modern innovations, the island's desserts provide both pleasure and insight, leaving visitors with lasting memories of La Palma's rich culinary heritage.

Chapter 7

Island Life

Villages and Towns

La Palma's charm is not only found in its dramatic landscapes and natural wonders but also in the character and authenticity of its villages and towns. Each settlement offers a unique glimpse into the island's history, architecture, and community life, from the colonial streets of Santa Cruz de La Palma to the quiet, traditional villages tucked into the valleys and mountains. Exploring these towns allows travelers to connect with the island's people, heritage, and daily rhythms, creating experiences that go beyond sightseeing and into the heart of La Palma's cultural identity.

Santa Cruz de La Palma, the island's capital, is a vibrant mix of history, culture, and modernity. Its streets are lined with colonial-era buildings adorned with wooden balconies, intricate facades, and colorful doors. Walking through the town center, visitors encounter plazas bustling with cafés, boutiques, and local markets, where the social pulse of the city is palpable. Santa Cruz also houses museums, art galleries, and historic churches, making it a hub for both cultural exploration and leisurely strolls. The blend of old-world charm and contemporary energy makes the capital a starting point for discovering the island's multifaceted identity.

Los Llanos de Aridane, located in the western part of La Palma, is another essential town to explore. Known for its lively commercial streets and central plazas, Los Llanos provides a more modern contrast to the colonial ambiance of Santa Cruz. Here, visitors can experience local shopping, cafés, and community life in an accessible, vibrant environment. The town is also a gateway to nearby natural attractions, making it convenient for those who want to balance urban experiences with outdoor adventures. Los Llanos embodies the practical, social, and cultural dimensions of La Palma's communities, showcasing a town that is both functional and inviting.

Smaller villages, such as Tazacorte, El Paso, and Puntallana, offer more intimate experiences and a closer connection to traditional island life. Tazacorte, with its black sand beaches and coastal charm, combines fishing heritage with modern amenities, providing a relaxed seaside atmosphere. El Paso, nestled in the central highlands, is surrounded by lush landscapes and agricultural terraces, reflecting La Palma's deep-rooted connection to farming and cultivation. Puntallana, with its cobblestone streets and colonial architecture, provides a sense of stepping back in time, where the slower pace of life allows for immersive observation of daily routines and local customs. Visiting these villages offers a contrast to the busier towns, highlighting the diversity of experiences available across the island.

Architecture plays a significant role in defining La Palma's villages and towns. Traditional Canarian houses, often painted in bright colors and featuring wooden balconies, coexist with modern constructions, reflecting the island's evolving identity. Narrow streets, plazas with fountains, and centuries-old churches create a sense of history and continuity. Public squares serve as gathering points where locals meet, children play, and markets or festivals take place. Observing the architecture and urban layout provides insight into the island's colonial past, social structure, and adaptation to the natural terrain.

Cultural life is woven into the fabric of each town. Festivals, religious celebrations, and public events are common, offering travelers a glimpse into local traditions. Street performances, music, and dance are often part of town celebrations, allowing visitors to participate or simply enjoy the vibrant atmosphere. Towns and villages function as living museums where history, culture, and daily life intersect, providing a multi-layered experience that extends beyond architecture and scenery.

Markets in towns and villages are particularly revealing of local culture. Farmers bring fresh produce, cheeses, honey, and tropical fruits to town centers, while artisans display crafts, textiles, and pottery. These markets are places of interaction, where travelers can taste local delicacies, purchase handmade items, and converse with residents who take pride in their traditions. Participating in these market activities provides a hands-on way to experience the economy, flavors, and creativity of La Palma's communities.

Scenic views and natural surroundings enhance the appeal of towns and villages. Many settlements are perched on hillsides or nestled in valleys, offering breathtaking vistas of mountains, forests, and the ocean. Walking through these towns often involves ascending cobbled streets or climbing gentle slopes, with rewarding panoramic views at each turn. These perspectives allow visitors to appreciate the interplay between human settlement and natural landscapes, a defining feature of La Palma's charm.

Local cuisine is also central to town life. Cafés, tapas bars, and family-run restaurants serve regional dishes, incorporating fresh ingredients sourced from nearby farms, rivers, and coasts. Dining in these establishments allows travelers to experience the tastes, aromas, and social customs of the island firsthand. Meals become cultural encounters, providing insight into local traditions, seasonal ingredients, and the communal spirit that defines La Palma's culinary culture.

Ultimately, exploring La Palma's villages and towns offers a layered, immersive experience. Each settlement carries its own story, shaped by geography, history, and the people who call it home. From bustling markets and lively plazas to quiet alleys and panoramic viewpoints, the towns and villages of La Palma invite visitors to slow down, observe, and engage. They provide a sense of connection, grounding the island's natural wonders and adventurous activities in the rich tapestry of human life, making every visit both memorable and meaningful.

Daily Routines

Experiencing La Palma through the lens of its daily routines offers a unique perspective on island life. Beyond the breathtaking landscapes, adventurous activities, and cultural landmarks, it is the rhythm of everyday living that gives the island its authenticity and charm. Observing how locals start their day, interact in public spaces, work, and relax provides travelers with a deeper understanding of La Palma's identity. These routines are shaped by the island's geography, climate, and traditions, creating a lifestyle that blends practicality, leisure, and community interaction in harmonious ways.

Mornings on La Palma often begin with a sense of calm and purpose. In towns and villages, the streets gradually awaken as locals open their shops, bakeries, and cafés. The aroma of freshly baked bread, pastries, and brewing coffee permeates the air, signaling the start of the day. Many residents stop at their neighborhood café for a quick espresso or café con leche paired with a sweet treat, such as bienmesabe or a trucha de batata. These morning rituals provide not only nourishment but also a moment for social interaction, as neighbors exchange greetings and news before embarking on their daily tasks.

Work routines on La Palma are influenced by the island's economy, which includes agriculture, tourism, small-scale commerce, and public services. Farmers often start early, tending to banana plantations, vineyards, and vegetable plots in the fertile valleys. Their work is physically demanding yet rhythmic, dictated by the cycles of planting, harvesting, and maintaining crops. In urban areas, shopkeepers, artisans, and office workers follow structured schedules, balancing customer service, production, and administration. Observing these routines reveals the dedication and adaptability of the island's workforce, who maintain a connection to both tradition and modernity.

School routines are another aspect of daily life, and they shape the atmosphere of towns and villages during the day. Children attend classes in local schools, and the streets around these institutions come alive with energy as families accompany them in the mornings and afternoons. The presence of schools also affects nearby cafés, markets, and public spaces, creating a dynamic flow of people and activity. For travelers, noticing these rhythms provides a sense of the community's priorities and the intergenerational continuity that sustains La Palma's social fabric.

Lunchtime is often a communal and leisurely affair. Many locals return home to enjoy meals with family, while others visit restaurants and cafés for a midday menu del día—a set lunch featuring fresh, seasonal ingredients, often including seafood, meats, vegetables, and local staples like papas arrugadas with mojo. Eating slowly, engaging in conversation, and savoring flavors are integral to this daily ritual, reflecting a lifestyle that values connection, sustenance, and enjoyment over mere convenience. Travelers who join in these routines gain insight into the social and culinary rhythms that structure life on the island.

Afternoons bring a slower pace, particularly in smaller towns and villages. Residents may rest, engage in hobbies, or enjoy outdoor activities such as walking, gardening, or visiting coastal areas. This period of rest and reflection is a hallmark of Canarian culture, allowing people to recharge before evening activities. For travelers, afternoons provide opportunities to explore quieter streets, observe everyday interactions, and notice details of architecture, public spaces, and community life that are often overlooked during busier hours.

Evenings on La Palma are often marked by social gatherings and leisure. Families and friends meet in plazas, cafés, or restaurants to share dinner, conversation, and entertainment. Outdoor terraces come alive with music, laughter, and the soft glow of streetlights, creating an inviting atmosphere for both locals and visitors. Nighttime routines may include walks along the coast, participation in local cultural events, or simply enjoying the cool breeze and serene surroundings. These evening activities reflect the islanders' emphasis on community, relaxation, and enjoyment of their natural and built environment.

Markets and shops often have their own daily rhythm, opening in the mornings to sell fresh produce, artisanal goods, and crafts, then closing or slowing in the afternoon before a final evening rush. Observing the ebb and flow of these spaces provides insight into economic activity, social interaction, and the integration of tradition with contemporary commerce. Travelers can engage with these routines by shopping alongside locals, tasting fresh foods, and asking questions about production methods and customs.

Transportation routines are also an important part of daily life. Buses, taxis, and cars follow predictable patterns, connecting villages, towns, and natural attractions. Cyclists and pedestrians share pathways in more rural areas, emphasizing the practical yet sustainable approaches to mobility on the island. Understanding these routines helps travelers navigate La Palma efficiently while appreciating the local approach to connectivity and movement.

Ultimately, observing daily routines in La Palma reveals the underlying rhythm that gives the island its character. From early morning cafés and agricultural work to leisurely afternoons and lively evening gatherings, each aspect of daily life is interconnected with community, culture, and environment. For visitors, paying attention to these patterns provides a richer, more immersive experience, allowing them to feel the pulse of the island beyond its tourist attractions. By integrating into these rhythms, travelers gain an authentic perspective on La Palma, one that celebrates both the simplicity and the depth of everyday life on this extraordinary island.

Festivals and Local Events

La Palma's vibrant culture comes alive through its festivals and local events, which provide travelers with an authentic glimpse into the island's traditions, community spirit, and lively social life. These celebrations, rooted in religious, historical, and agricultural customs, are opportunities to witness the richness of Canarian culture firsthand. From colorful parades and street parties to intimate village rituals, each event carries a sense of identity and belonging, revealing the heart and soul of La Palma's communities.

One of the most notable celebrations is the Fiesta de la Bajada de la Virgen, which occurs in Santa Cruz de La Palma. This event, held every five years, honors the island's patron saint and is characterized by elaborate processions, traditional music, and folkloric dances. Residents and visitors alike participate in decorating streets, creating intricate floral displays, and preparing traditional foods. The festival is both a religious and social occasion, drawing communities together in celebration while showcasing centuries-old customs. Attending such an event allows travelers to appreciate the depth of devotion and the communal energy that defines island life.

Smaller towns and villages also host their own annual fiestas, often tied to patron saints or historical anniversaries. These events typically include music, dancing, craft stalls, and culinary specialties, providing a full sensory experience of La Palma's culture. For example, villages in the northern and central parts of the island often organize traditional folk music performances, where local musicians play guitars, drums, and the timple—a small Canarian stringed instrument. Dance troupes perform traditional dances in colorful costumes, inviting participation from the audience and fostering a sense of inclusion and enjoyment. Such festivals highlight the living traditions that continue to shape the social fabric of the island.

Carnival celebrations are another highlight on La Palma, taking place in multiple towns during the pre-Lenten season. These carnivals are vibrant, playful, and highly creative, featuring parades with elaborate costumes, masks, and floats. Music, dancing, and street performances create an energetic and festive atmosphere, where locals and visitors come together to celebrate life and creativity. Carnival on La Palma is characterized by its community-driven spirit, with many groups spending months preparing costumes and performances, emphasizing collaboration, artistry, and a shared sense of joy.

Agricultural festivals celebrate the island's rich produce and culinary traditions. Events such as grape harvest festivals, banana fairs, and honey markets allow visitors to experience the agricultural heartbeat of La Palma. During these festivals, attendees can taste fresh fruits, sample local wines, and learn about traditional farming practices that have sustained the island for generations. These celebrations are both educational and festive, offering insight into how La Palma's natural bounty is integrated into daily life, cuisine, and cultural identity.

Music and dance feature prominently in local events. Traditional Canarian music, often performed live, creates an immersive cultural environment. Audiences may hear rhythmic percussion, melodic strings, and harmonious vocals, while dancers in traditional attire perform intricate steps passed down through generations. These performances often occur in town squares, village streets, or community centers, making the experience accessible and engaging for all ages. Visitors have the opportunity to observe, participate, and even learn a few steps, deepening their connection to the island's living traditions.

Religious events and processions are another cornerstone of La Palma's cultural calendar. Holy Week, Christmas celebrations, and other religious observances are marked by solemn yet vibrant rituals, combining spiritual devotion with public spectacle. Processions feature statues, floral decorations, candles, and music, often accompanied by community members dressed in ceremonial attire. These events provide a glimpse into the enduring faith and shared values that have shaped La Palma's identity, highlighting the blend of reverence, pageantry, and communal pride that characterizes island life.

Local markets and fairs are often integrated into festival celebrations, creating a lively hub of commerce, socializing, and cultural exchange. Artisans, food vendors, and performers fill streets and plazas, offering everything from handcrafted goods to traditional dishes and sweets. These spaces encourage interaction between locals and travelers, allowing visitors to engage with the community, learn about local crafts, and sample regional flavors. The combination of festivities, commerce, and social activity ensures a multi-dimensional cultural experience that is both memorable and educational.

Seasonal events, such as the celebration of San Juan in June, highlight the importance of natural cycles and celestial phenomena in La Palma's traditions. Bonfires, music, and communal gatherings mark the arrival of summer, blending pagan and Christian influences into a vibrant social and cultural ritual. These events emphasize the islanders' connection to nature, the land, and the changing seasons, creating experiences that resonate with both residents and visitors. Participating in these seasonal celebrations provides insight into the values, beliefs, and creative expression of La Palma's communities.

Ultimately, festivals and local events are essential to understanding La Palma beyond its landscapes and tourist attractions. They reveal the island's living culture, the importance of community, and the depth of tradition that shapes daily life. By engaging with these celebrations, travelers gain a richer, more immersive perspective on the island, creating memories of music, dance, food, and human connection that last long after the event has ended. Experiencing La Palma through its festivals transforms a visit into a participatory journey, blending observation with active engagement in the island's vibrant cultural tapestry.

Chapter 8

Hidden Gems

Secret Viewpoints

La Palma is often called "La Isla Bonita" for good reason, and one of the best ways to appreciate its beauty is by discovering the island's secret viewpoints. While popular miradores offer stunning panoramas, the true magic often lies in hidden spots tucked away from the main tourist trails. These secret viewpoints provide moments of serenity, uninterrupted vistas, and an intimate connection with La Palma's dramatic landscapes, making them essential stops for travelers seeking a deeper, more personal experience of the island.

One of the defining features of La Palma's topography is its dramatic elevation changes. From steep volcanic ridges to deep ravines and lush valleys, the island's terrain creates countless natural lookout points. Many of these viewpoints are accessible only via hiking trails, narrow paths, or quiet village streets, ensuring a sense of discovery and exclusivity. Travelers who venture off the beaten path are rewarded with perspectives that capture the interplay of mountains, forests, and the Atlantic Ocean in ways that are often overlooked by casual sightseeing.

The Caldera de Taburiente National Park is home to some of the island's most breathtaking secret viewpoints. Beyond the main observation points, hidden ledges and ridge trails reveal striking vistas of cascading valleys, dense pine forests, and the caldera's rugged cliffs. Early morning hikes often reward visitors with mist rising from the forest floors, softening the landscape and creating a mystical atmosphere. These moments of quiet reflection offer both photographers and nature enthusiasts the chance to capture La Palma's raw beauty in its most unspoiled form.

Coastal cliffs and headlands also host secluded viewpoints that reveal the contrast between La Palma's lush interior and its volcanic shoreline.

Paths along the western and northern coasts lead to small promontories where visitors can witness waves crashing against black volcanic rocks, seabirds gliding on the wind, and the sun setting over the Atlantic. These locations are often devoid of crowds, providing a sense of solitude and connection to nature that enhances the visual spectacle. Observing the ocean from these vantage points reminds travelers of the island's maritime heritage and the power of its surrounding waters.

Some secret viewpoints are tucked within small villages or rural areas. Walking through narrow alleys or ascending unmarked trails often leads to terraces, rooftop gardens, or secluded plazas that overlook valleys, mountains, and the ocean. These locations offer unique perspectives of daily life unfolding below, with terraced farms, colorful rooftops, and winding streets forming a tapestry of human habitation intertwined with the natural environment. Engaging with these village viewpoints allows visitors to see La Palma as locals do, appreciating the scale and intimacy of its settlements.

Sunrise and sunset experiences are particularly memorable from secret viewpoints. The island's western cliffs and elevated ridges are perfect for watching the sun dip below the horizon, casting golden light over volcanic peaks and valleys. In contrast, eastern vantage points capture the first light illuminating misty forests and terraced fields, revealing textures and colors invisible during midday. These moments of transition highlight the island's dynamic beauty and provide photographers, painters, and travelers with an ever-changing canvas of light and shadow.

For those seeking adventure, many secret viewpoints are accessible only via off-the-map trails or less-traveled hiking paths. Exploring these routes requires preparation, awareness, and respect for the environment, but the rewards are unparalleled. Visitors often find isolated benches, rock outcroppings, or quiet clearings that allow for meditation, reflection, or simply absorbing the grandeur of La Palma. The sense of discovery adds an emotional dimension to the visual experience, making these hidden spots feel like personal treasures.

Birdwatchers and wildlife enthusiasts also benefit from these secret locations. Many viewpoints provide unobstructed observation of endemic birds, lizards, and other wildlife. The elevated positions and minimal human interference create ideal conditions for spotting species in their natural habitats. This connection with the island's fauna adds another layer to the experience, highlighting La Palma's ecological diversity alongside its scenic beauty.

Local knowledge often guides visitors to the best secret viewpoints. Conversations with residents, tips from hikers, or information from small village cafés can lead to hidden gems unknown to guidebooks or mainstream maps. These insights create opportunities for cultural exchange, storytelling, and a more immersive travel experience. By seeking out these locations with guidance from locals, travelers not only find spectacular vistas but also participate in the living culture of La Palma.

Ultimately, La Palma's secret viewpoints offer more than just scenic vistas—they provide moments of reflection, inspiration, and connection. Whether perched on a remote cliff, tucked within a quiet village, or hidden along a forest trail, these locations invite travelers to pause, observe, and appreciate the island's intricate beauty. Experiencing La Palma from these unique perspectives transforms sightseeing into a personal journey, leaving lasting impressions of the island's landscapes, light, and life.

Off-the-Beaten-Path Spots

La Palma's true essence often reveals itself away from the well-trodden paths, in places where tranquility, authenticity, and breathtaking beauty coexist without the interruption of crowds. While the island's main viewpoints, trails, and coastal areas attract visitors for good reason, it is the off-the-beaten-path spots that offer a more intimate, immersive, and memorable experience. These hidden corners allow travelers to connect with the island's landscapes, history, and local life on a deeper level, discovering aspects of La Palma that are overlooked by most guidebooks.

One of the charms of exploring off-the-beaten-path locations is the sense of discovery. Narrow mountain trails, winding rural roads, and secluded coastal paths lead to vistas, waterfalls, and natural pools that remain relatively untouched. For hikers, these trails often require patience, stamina, and careful navigation, but the rewards are immense: panoramic views of volcanic craters, dense forests, and sparkling Atlantic waters unfold in dramatic fashion, offering both solitude and inspiration. Travelers who venture beyond popular routes are often the only ones enjoying these spaces, providing a rare feeling of exclusivity and peace.

The island's interior is particularly rich in hidden treasures. Remote hamlets like Garafía and Puntallana are characterized by terraced landscapes, traditional architecture, and narrow streets where local life continues largely undisturbed. Visitors who explore these villages can witness daily routines—farmers tending to crops, locals gathering at small cafés, and artisans crafting traditional goods—offering a vivid glimpse into La Palma's cultural heartbeat. These settlements serve as living museums where every corner tells a story, from centuries-old churches to centuries-old stone walls that guide terraces along steep slopes.

Water lovers are rewarded with secluded coastal spots that are often overlooked. Black sand beaches, volcanic rock pools, and hidden coves along the western and northern shores provide opportunities for swimming, snorkeling, or simply relaxing in privacy. Some of these locations require careful navigation or short hikes to reach, but the combination of dramatic cliffs, unspoiled beaches, and the soothing sound of the Atlantic waves creates an unforgettable experience. Observing marine life from these vantage points also highlights the island's ecological diversity, making it a haven for nature enthusiasts.

Volcanic landscapes are central to La Palma's identity, and off-the-beaten-path trails reveal features unseen by casual tourists. Lava fields, dormant craters, and rocky ridges are scattered across the island, often accessible via narrow trails or unmarked paths. Hikers and photographers are particularly drawn to these locations for the dramatic interplay of light, texture, and shadow. The rugged terrain serves as a reminder of the island's volcanic origins, adding a sense of history and raw natural power to the adventure of exploration.

Forest walks in the island's interior are another highlight for those seeking less crowded experiences. The laurel forests of Los Tilos and other protected areas contain winding paths, moss-covered trees, and hidden streams. Walking these trails provides a multisensory experience: the scent of damp earth and foliage, the sound of water trickling through rocks, and the occasional rustle of endemic wildlife. Off-the-beaten-path exploration in these areas allows visitors to truly immerse themselves in La Palma's natural ecosystems, far from the distractions of urban life or tourist hubs.

Hidden viewpoints within the interior and coastal areas offer perspectives that feel entirely personal. Unlike well-known miradores, these spots often require patience and a sense of curiosity, but the reward is a moment of quiet reflection and awe. Observing the island's mountains, valleys, and ocean expanses from a secluded perch encourages mindfulness and a deeper appreciation for the scale and diversity of La Palma's landscapes. Photographers, writers, and nature enthusiasts often find these off-the-beaten-path locations ideal for capturing unique, untouched perspectives of the island.

Cultural off-the-beaten-path experiences are equally compelling. Small local festivals, artisan workshops, and community gatherings often occur in villages that see few tourists. Participating in these events allows travelers to observe traditional dances, crafts, and culinary practices in an authentic setting. Engaging with locals in such intimate spaces fosters meaningful connections, creating memories that are as rich culturally as they are visually. These experiences highlight the depth of La Palma's heritage and the warmth of its people.

Seasonal changes further enhance the allure of hidden spots. Wildflower blooms, migrating birds, and changing foliage colors transform familiar landscapes into entirely new vistas. Observing these shifts in less frequented areas provides a more personal encounter with the island's rhythms, revealing patterns of life and nature that might go unnoticed in crowded tourist areas. Being attuned to these subtle transformations deepens the sense of connection with La Palma's environment and its cyclical beauty.

Ultimately, La Palma's off-the-beaten-path spots reward curiosity, patience, and a willingness to explore. They offer solitude, discovery, and immersive experiences that reveal the island's hidden dimensions—its quiet villages, secret beaches, lush forests, volcanic wonders, and authentic cultural expressions. Traveling beyond the obvious destinations allows visitors to see La Palma as locals do, experiencing the rhythms, textures, and beauty that make the island truly extraordinary. These hidden gems transform a visit from a typical sightseeing trip into a personal journey of exploration and wonder.

Local Stories

La Palma's landscapes and daily life are imbued with stories passed down through generations, providing travelers with a deeper understanding of the island's character, culture, and history. These local tales, legends, and personal anecdotes transform ordinary streets, mountains, and villages into living narratives, connecting visitors to the people who have shaped the island over centuries. By listening, observing, and engaging with these stories, travelers gain insight into the heart of La Palma, where natural wonders, historical events, and communal memory intertwine.

Many local stories revolve around La Palma's dramatic geography and volcanic origins. The island's volcanoes, craters, and lava flows have inspired myths and legends explaining their formation, the spirits that dwell within them, and their influence on human life. Tales of fiery eruptions and mysterious volcanic phenomena are often shared by elders in small villages, passed on as warnings, moral lessons, or simply entertainment. These narratives provide a cultural lens through which the island's dramatic natural features are not only observed but also understood, giving a human dimension to the rugged landscape.

Historical stories also abound, reflecting La Palma's complex past. From early Guanche inhabitants to Spanish colonization and maritime trade, the island's history is woven into its villages, churches, and streets. Travelers may learn about legendary figures, heroic acts, or events that shaped communities during excursions through towns like Santa Cruz de La Palma or Los Llanos de Aridane. Visiting historic sites with the context of these stories transforms monuments and buildings from static structures into symbols of human resilience, creativity, and continuity.

Maritime stories are particularly prominent on La Palma, given its island location. Tales of fishermen, sailors, and shipwrecks abound, reflecting the community's longstanding connection to the Atlantic Ocean. These stories describe both triumph and tragedy, capturing the risks and rewards of life at sea. Many local fishermen continue to share these accounts, providing not only historical insight but also lessons about courage, perseverance, and respect for nature. Coastal villages, ports, and harbors become more than picturesque stops—they become storytellers' stages where history and human experience merge.

Folklore and supernatural tales are deeply embedded in La Palma's villages and forests. Legends of spirits, enchanted forests, and mysterious creatures enrich the cultural tapestry, particularly in rural areas where oral tradition remains strong. Children grow up hearing stories of local heroes, witches, or magical beings associated with natural landmarks. For visitors, these tales add layers of intrigue and imagination, making hikes through laurel forests or walks along volcanic ridges feel like journeys into both nature and myth. Engaging with these stories fosters curiosity and offers a unique perspective on the island's cultural psyche.

Local artisans, musicians, and performers often serve as carriers of the island's stories. Through songs, dances, and craft-making, they preserve and communicate historical events, legends, and social values. For example, traditional folk music performed at festivals or village gatherings often recounts heroic deeds, romantic tales, or humorous anecdotes. Handcrafted items may incorporate symbols, motifs, or stories that reflect community values or historical narratives. Interacting with these creators allows travelers to experience La Palma's history and culture in a tangible, participatory way.

Personal anecdotes and contemporary stories add a human dimension to the island experience. Residents frequently share tales of family life, local traditions, or personal encounters with visitors, creating connections that go beyond sightseeing. These stories provide insight into daily life, challenges, and joys on La Palma, offering context for the island's culture, economy, and social fabric. Listening to these accounts allows travelers to perceive the island as a living community rather than simply a destination, deepening both understanding and empathy.

Historical commemorations and festivals also serve as repositories of local stories. Parades, religious ceremonies, and community events often reference significant moments in the island's past, from victories and migrations to natural disasters and acts of heroism. Participating in these events provides an immersive opportunity to witness stories brought to life through performance, ritual, and collective memory. Travelers gain a sense of continuity, seeing how past narratives inform contemporary culture and community identity.

Hidden corners of towns, villages, and natural landscapes often hold stories waiting to be discovered. Plaques on historic buildings, inscriptions in churches, and monuments scattered across the island tell of events and individuals who shaped La Palma. Exploring these details rewards attentive travelers with narratives that enrich understanding, turning casual exploration into a more meaningful journey. Even a simple walk down a quiet street can reveal stories of the past intertwined with the present, offering layers of history and human experience.

Ultimately, La Palma's local stories transform the island from a scenic destination into a living cultural landscape. Each tale, legend, or anecdote adds depth, context, and emotion to the natural beauty, architecture, and community life. Engaging with these narratives allows travelers to see the island through the eyes of its people, experiencing not only what is visible but also what is felt, remembered, and imagined. Local stories create lasting connections, turning a visit to La Palma into a journey of understanding, empathy, and wonder that lingers long after departure.

Chapter 9

Shopping & Souvenirs

Markets and Boutiques

La Palma's charm extends beyond its landscapes and villages to the vibrant markets and quaint boutiques that give travelers a glimpse into local life, commerce, and creativity. These spaces are more than shopping destinations—they are cultural hubs where residents gather, traditions are preserved, and visitors can experience the flavors, craftsmanship, and energy of the island firsthand. Exploring markets and boutiques offers insights into La Palma's economy, artisanal heritage, and daily rhythms, transforming shopping into an immersive cultural experience.

The island's weekly markets are a central feature of community life. In towns such as Santa Cruz de La Palma and Los Llanos de Aridane, morning markets fill public squares with colorful stalls selling fresh produce, tropical fruits, local cheeses, and artisanal baked goods. Farmers and producers often arrive early to display their harvests, ensuring quality and freshness. For travelers, these markets provide a sensory feast: the scent of freshly baked bread, the vivid colors of papayas and bananas, and the sound of lively bargaining create an authentic Canarian atmosphere. Visiting a market is also an opportunity to engage with locals, learn about seasonal produce, and understand the island's agricultural cycles.

Beyond food, markets feature a variety of handmade crafts, textiles, and souvenirs that reflect La Palma's cultural heritage. Artisans display ceramics, woven baskets, embroidery, and jewelry, often crafted using traditional techniques passed down through generations. These items carry both aesthetic and cultural value, offering travelers tangible connections to the island's artistic traditions. By browsing and purchasing from local artisans, visitors support small-scale economies and gain unique mementos that cannot be found elsewhere.

Specialty markets, often tied to festivals or seasonal events, provide a deeper look into the island's creativity and culinary prowess. For instance, honey festivals, wine fairs, and artisan craft markets allow travelers to explore La Palma's diverse products and learn about their origins. Tastings, demonstrations, and workshops are common, offering hands-on experiences that go beyond passive observation. These markets celebrate local ingenuity, highlight sustainable production, and foster connections between producers and consumers, creating a rich cultural exchange.

Boutiques in towns and villages complement the island's markets by offering curated selections of fashion, homeware, and specialty items. Many boutiques feature clothing and accessories designed by local artists, often incorporating traditional patterns, natural fibers, and sustainable materials. Shopping in these small establishments allows visitors to discover products that reflect La Palma's identity, style, and artisanal culture. Boutique owners are usually eager to share the stories behind their merchandise, creating a personalized shopping experience that connects consumers with the creators.

Antique and specialty shops provide another dimension to La Palma's retail landscape. These stores often house rare objects, vintage furniture, and collectibles that reveal the island's history and aesthetic sensibilities. Exploring these spaces allows travelers to uncover pieces of the past, whether through restored furnishings, old photographs, or handcrafted instruments. Such discoveries enrich understanding of La Palma's cultural evolution and offer unique opportunities for meaningful purchases that carry historical significance.

For those seeking culinary souvenirs, markets and boutiques provide an array of options. Locally produced wines, cheeses, preserves, and sweets such as bienmesabe or truchas de batata can be purchased to enjoy later or gift to loved ones. Specialty shops often emphasize quality and authenticity, sourcing directly from local farms or small producers. Sampling and selecting these products in their place of origin adds context and appreciation, creating lasting memories linked to the flavors and traditions of the island.

Exploring markets and boutiques also reveals the rhythm of daily life on La Palma. Early mornings bustle with activity as vendors set up stalls and residents shop for fresh ingredients. Afternoons are quieter, allowing travelers to browse leisurely, observe interactions, and absorb the ambiance. Evenings often bring socializing, as cafés and small eateries near markets become gathering points for friends and families. Engaging with these spaces at different times of day provides insight into the local tempo, social habits, and cultural priorities.

Cultural exchange is another key element of La Palma's markets and boutiques. Travelers often have the chance to converse with vendors, learn about production techniques, and gain stories behind the goods. These interactions are more than transactional—they are educational and personal, fostering connections between visitors and locals. Understanding the context of what is sold, how it is made, and its significance within the community enriches the shopping experience, making it both meaningful and memorable.

Ultimately, La Palma's markets and boutiques are windows into the island's soul. They reveal the creativity, tradition, and daily life of its people, offering visitors experiences that go beyond sightseeing. From bustling produce markets and artisan fairs to curated boutiques and specialty shops, these spaces invite exploration, curiosity, and engagement. Discovering La Palma through its local commerce provides a unique lens on culture, heritage, and community, leaving travelers with both tangible souvenirs and intangible memories that capture the spirit of the island.

Handmade Treasures

La Palma is a haven for handmade treasures, where artisanal skill, creativity, and tradition converge to create objects that reflect the island's culture, history, and natural beauty. From intricate ceramics and woven textiles to locally crafted jewelry and woodwork, these treasures offer travelers a tangible connection to La Palma's heritage. Exploring the island's handmade goods provides insight into the ingenuity and craftsmanship of its people, turning shopping into a journey of discovery and appreciation.

Artisans across the island continue to work with techniques passed down through generations, preserving cultural identity while adapting to contemporary tastes. Ceramics are a notable example, with workshops producing pottery that blends traditional Canarian forms with modern designs. Plates, vases, and decorative pieces often feature motifs inspired by La Palma's volcanic landscapes, endemic flora, and maritime heritage. Visiting these workshops allows travelers to witness the creative process firsthand, from shaping the clay to the careful application of glaze and patterns, offering a deeper appreciation of the labor and artistry involved.

Textile production is another vibrant facet of the island's handmade culture. Local weavers create rugs, wall hangings, and clothing using natural fibers such as wool and cotton, often dyed with colors inspired by the surrounding landscapes. Traditional patterns and techniques are preserved, yet artisans experiment with new designs to appeal to modern buyers. Small boutiques and craft fairs showcase these textiles, allowing visitors to admire the skill involved and select pieces that carry both functional and aesthetic value. Each item tells a story, reflecting the history, identity, and creativity of its maker.

Jewelry and accessory crafting on La Palma often incorporates materials sourced from the island itself, such as volcanic stones, shells, and wood. Artisans skillfully transform these natural elements into rings, necklaces, bracelets, and hairpieces that capture the essence of La Palma. Each piece embodies a connection to the island's environment and heritage, offering travelers souvenirs that are both beautiful and meaningful. Many jewelry makers are happy to share the inspiration and techniques behind their creations, enhancing the visitor's understanding and engagement.

Woodworking is another traditional craft that thrives on La Palma. Skilled carpenters create furniture, kitchenware, decorative items, and toys, often using local wood species. The finished pieces balance functionality and artistry, reflecting centuries of craftsmanship adapted to modern life. Visiting small workshops or village stores allows travelers to observe the tools, techniques, and dedication involved in woodworking, providing an appreciation of the meticulous attention to detail that defines La Palma's handmade culture.

Markets and artisan fairs are excellent venues for discovering these handmade treasures. Stalls brimming with colorful ceramics, woven fabrics, and handcrafted jewelry create a lively and inspiring atmosphere. Many artisans demonstrate their techniques on-site, inviting visitors to engage with the creative process. These events are often accompanied by music, traditional food, and storytelling, enriching the shopping experience with cultural immersion. Travelers gain more than souvenirs—they gain insight into the artistic traditions and daily lives of La Palma's communities.

Gift shops and small boutiques complement markets by offering curated selections of handmade goods. Unlike mass-produced items, these treasures carry authenticity, individuality, and a personal touch.

Travelers can find items that reflect their experiences on the island, from a handcrafted vase inspired by volcanic formations to a woven textile capturing the colors of local forests. Each purchase becomes a memory, linking the object to a particular place, story, or encounter.

Cultural significance is embedded in many handmade items. Folk motifs, religious symbols, and references to local legends or history are often incorporated into designs, connecting the products to La Palma's heritage. Owning such items allows travelers to carry a piece of the island's identity home, while also supporting the preservation of these artistic traditions. By understanding the context and meaning behind the craftsmanship, visitors can appreciate the layers of culture woven into each creation.

Learning opportunities abound for travelers interested in hands-on experiences. Some artisans offer workshops or guided sessions where visitors can try their hand at pottery, weaving, or jewelry making. Participating in these activities deepens understanding of the craft, provides insight into the skills required, and creates a personal connection to the island's creative culture. Travelers leave not only with a handmade object but also with memories of the process and the knowledge that they contributed to the art themselves.

Ultimately, La Palma's handmade treasures offer more than aesthetic value—they are cultural ambassadors. Each piece tells a story of creativity, heritage, and connection to the island's environment and people. From workshops tucked away in villages to bustling artisan markets, these objects allow travelers to engage with La Palma's artistic soul, supporting local craftsmen and preserving traditions for future generations. Collecting, observing, or even creating these treasures enriches any journey to the island, turning shopping into a meaningful, immersive, and memorable experience.

What to Bring Home

One of the joys of traveling to La Palma is the opportunity to take a piece of the island home with you, whether as a souvenir, a gift, or a personal reminder of your journey. From artisanal crafts and local culinary delights to unique mementos inspired by the island's landscapes, La Palma offers a rich selection of items that reflect its culture, heritage, and natural beauty. Choosing what to bring home allows travelers to extend their experience beyond the trip, keeping memories alive while supporting local communities and traditions.

Culinary specialties are among the most cherished items to take from La Palma. The island's agricultural bounty includes fresh fruits, locally produced cheeses, honey, and wines, each with distinctive flavors tied to the volcanic soils and microclimates of the region. Papas arrugadas, or "wrinkled potatoes," are often accompanied by traditional sauces such as mojo rojo or mojo verde, which are available in bottled form. These culinary gifts allow travelers to recreate authentic island flavors in their own kitchens, sharing the taste of La Palma with friends and family.

La Palma's handmade crafts also make meaningful souvenirs. Ceramics, woven textiles, and wooden carvings are not only beautiful but also carry the stories, techniques, and heritage of local artisans. Handcrafted items such as timple-inspired decorations, embroidered linens, and intricately designed pottery provide both decorative and functional value. Purchasing these products supports small businesses while allowing travelers to own objects imbued with the island's artistic spirit, making each piece a unique reminder of their visit.

Jewelry and accessories crafted on La Palma are popular choices for travelers seeking something personal and elegant. Many pieces incorporate volcanic stones, seashells, or locally sourced wood, reflecting the island's natural environment. Necklaces, bracelets, rings, and hairpieces often showcase traditional designs adapted with modern sensibilities, creating wearable art that carries cultural significance. These treasures serve as both fashionable adornments and keepsakes, connecting the wearer to the landscapes and culture of La Palma.

For visitors interested in souvenirs with cultural depth, books, prints, and artwork are excellent options. Local artists capture the island's landscapes, seascapes, and wildlife in paintings, photographs, and prints that convey both beauty and emotion. Guidebooks, local history volumes, or collections of folk tales allow travelers to delve deeper into La Palma's heritage, providing knowledge and context that enrich the memory of their journey. These intellectual and artistic keepsakes are especially meaningful for those who appreciate cultural immersion.

Specialty food products such as local sweets and preserves also make delightful gifts. Treats like truchas de batata, bienmesabe, and almond-based confections are often packaged to travel easily, offering a taste of La Palma's culinary tradition long after leaving the island. Olive oils, vinegars, and artisanal jams are also popular, reflecting both flavor and the care of local production. Sharing these items with others introduces friends and family to La Palma's distinctive tastes and culinary heritage.

Markets and artisan fairs are ideal places to discover what to bring home. Browsing stalls brimming with crafts, jewelry, and local produce allows travelers to explore a variety of options in one location, while conversations with vendors provide insight into the stories and techniques behind each item. These interactions enhance the value of souvenirs, as travelers gain a sense of connection to the people who made them, turning purchases into meaningful mementos rather than mere commercial transactions.

For environmentally conscious travelers, La Palma offers sustainable souvenir options. Many artisans use natural, locally sourced materials and eco-friendly techniques, from recycled wood and volcanic stone to organic dyes and fibers. Supporting these products promotes responsible tourism while allowing visitors to bring home items that align with their values. Choosing sustainable souvenirs also reflects an appreciation for the island's delicate ecosystems and the importance of preserving its natural beauty for future generations.

Personalized or customized items add an extra layer of significance. Some boutiques and workshops offer the option to engrave, paint, or otherwise personalize crafts, jewelry, or textiles. These customizations create one-of-a-kind keepsakes that commemorate the trip in a uniquely meaningful way. Travelers can commemorate special occasions, mark milestones, or simply create a memento that resonates with their personal experience on the island.

Ultimately, what to bring home from La Palma goes beyond mere souvenirs—it is an extension of the travel experience itself. Each item tells a story, preserves a memory, and supports the local culture and economy. From artisanal crafts and culinary specialties to artwork, jewelry, and sustainable products, the island offers a wealth of choices that capture its beauty, heritage, and spirit. Bringing these treasures home allows travelers to continue their connection with La Palma, sharing its essence with others while keeping the magic of the island alive long after the journey ends.

Chapter 10

Practical Tips

Safety and Health

Traveling to La Palma is an exciting adventure, but ensuring personal safety and maintaining good health is essential for a smooth and enjoyable experience. The island is generally safe for visitors, with low crime rates and welcoming communities, yet awareness and preparation can prevent common travel mishaps and enhance your overall journey. Understanding local conditions, health precautions, and safety practices allows travelers to fully enjoy La Palma's landscapes, activities, and culture with peace of mind.

Health considerations begin with routine preparation. Visitors should ensure that vaccinations are up to date, including standard immunizations like tetanus, diphtheria, and influenza. While La Palma does not pose unusual health risks, travelers with specific medical conditions should carry prescriptions and medical documentation. A small travel health kit is advisable, containing essentials such as pain relievers, antihistamines, bandages, and antiseptics. This preparation allows for prompt treatment of minor injuries or discomforts encountered during hiking, exploring villages, or visiting remote areas.

The island's outdoor activities, from hiking volcanic trails to exploring forests and coastal areas, present both opportunities and risks. Hikers should wear sturdy footwear, carry sufficient water, and use sun protection, as exposure to the sun at higher altitudes can be intense. Weather conditions can change quickly in mountainous areas, so layers, rain protection, and a reliable map or GPS are recommended. By being prepared for environmental challenges, travelers can minimize the risk of accidents, dehydration, or exposure-related issues.

Water safety is also important, particularly for those exploring beaches, cliffs, or engaging in water sports. While La Palma's beaches are generally safe, ocean currents and wave conditions can vary. Paying attention to local advice, warning signs, and lifeguard instructions is essential, especially in less populated or off-the-beaten-path locations. Wearing life jackets during kayaking, snorkeling, or other water activities enhances safety, while basic knowledge of swimming and self-rescue techniques can prevent accidents.

Food and drink safety should be considered, although La Palma maintains high standards for hygiene and sanitation. Tap water is generally safe to drink, yet travelers with sensitive stomachs may prefer bottled water. Sampling local cuisine is part of the island experience, but it is wise to eat at reputable restaurants, markets, or cafés to minimize the risk of foodborne illness. Travelers should also be mindful of allergies or dietary restrictions, asking about ingredients and preparation methods when necessary.

Emergency services on La Palma are reliable and accessible. Police, medical facilities, and fire services operate throughout the island, and emergency numbers are standard across Spain (112 for all emergencies). Knowing the locations of nearby hospitals, clinics, and pharmacies before venturing into remote areas is helpful, as some hiking trails or coastal spots are distant from immediate assistance. Keeping a charged mobile phone and sharing travel plans with companions or local contacts further enhances safety.

Personal safety practices include vigilance in public spaces and respect for local regulations. Petty theft is rare but possible in tourist areas, so securing valuables, using hotel safes, and being cautious with belongings is prudent. Respecting local laws, signage, and cultural norms ensures positive interactions and avoids misunderstandings. Night travel, especially in less populated areas, should be approached with caution, and using trusted transportation options contributes to overall security.

Travelers engaging in adventure activities should prioritize professional guidance and appropriate equipment. Guided hikes, organized tours, and certified instructors for climbing, diving, or kayaking reduce risk and provide educational insight into the island's natural features. Understanding the physical demands of activities, assessing personal fitness, and pacing oneself prevents exhaustion, injuries, or strain. Combining preparation with expert advice ensures that La Palma's adventurous offerings remain enjoyable rather than hazardous.

Health insurance coverage is an essential precaution for all travelers. Comprehensive travel insurance that includes medical care, evacuation, and coverage for adventure sports is recommended. Knowing the terms of your insurance, including local healthcare providers and claim procedures, provides peace of mind and financial protection in case of unexpected incidents. Additionally, carrying identification and health information in case of emergencies facilitates prompt and accurate medical attention.

Ultimately, prioritizing safety and health allows visitors to fully immerse themselves in La Palma's landscapes, culture, and experiences. From understanding environmental conditions and water safety to maintaining good hygiene, preparing for medical needs, and following personal security practices, careful planning ensures that the island's natural beauty and vibrant communities can be explored with confidence. Being proactive about safety and health transforms a trip into a secure, enjoyable, and memorable journey, letting travelers focus on the wonders of La Palma rather than worries or preventable risks.

Money Matters

Managing finances effectively while traveling on La Palma is crucial to ensure a smooth and enjoyable experience without unnecessary stress. While the island is relatively affordable compared to other

European destinations, being prepared with knowledge of local costs, currency options, payment methods, and budgeting strategies helps travelers make the most of their trip. Understanding money matters also enables visitors to engage comfortably in shopping, dining, excursions, and cultural experiences without unexpected surprises.

The official currency on La Palma is the Euro (EUR), and it is widely accepted across the island. Cash remains important for smaller establishments, markets, and remote areas where card payments may not be available. ATMs are conveniently located in towns, cities, and major tourist areas, providing access to cash when needed. Travelers should be aware of potential bank fees for withdrawals and consider withdrawing larger amounts to minimize charges, while keeping funds securely stored during excursions or day trips.

Credit and debit cards are widely accepted in hotels, larger restaurants, and retail stores, particularly in Santa Cruz de La Palma and Los Llanos de Aridane. Visa and Mastercard are the most commonly used, while American Express and other cards may be less widely accepted. Travelers should notify their banks of their travel plans to avoid card blocks and ensure they understand international transaction fees. Contactless payments and mobile wallets are increasingly accepted, offering convenience and security for small transactions.

Budgeting is an essential aspect of money management on La Palma. Daily expenses vary depending on activities, dining preferences, and accommodations. Eating at local cafés, purchasing fresh produce from markets, or enjoying picnic-style meals can be more affordable than frequent restaurant dining. Similarly, opting for public transport or rental vehicles over taxis can help manage transportation costs. Travelers who plan ahead for excursions, guided tours, and specialty activities can prevent overspending while still enjoying a full range of experiences.

Dining costs on La Palma can vary significantly depending on location and style. Traditional Canarian restaurants offer hearty meals at reasonable prices, while fine dining establishments in tourist areas may be more expensive. Local tapas bars, small cafés, and bakeries provide budget-friendly options for casual meals, snacks, or coffee breaks. Travelers can enjoy fresh seafood, tropical fruits, and island specialties without exceeding their budget by seeking out local recommendations and daily specials.

Shopping and souvenirs are another area where budgeting is important. Markets, artisan fairs, and boutiques offer unique handmade items, culinary treats, and crafts, but prices can vary widely. Comparing products, understanding local pricing norms, and prioritizing meaningful or high-quality purchases helps travelers maximize their spending. Additionally, some items may be cheaper in less touristy areas or when purchased directly from producers rather than through intermediaries.

Transportation costs include public buses, car rentals, and fuel if exploring the island independently. Public buses provide a cost-effective means of reaching major towns, villages, and some attractions. Renting a car offers flexibility, especially for accessing remote viewpoints and hiking trails, but fuel, insurance, and parking fees should be factored into the budget. Planning routes and combining destinations in a single trip helps optimize costs and time.

Travelers should also consider miscellaneous expenses such as entry fees for parks, guided tours, or cultural sites. While many of La Palma's natural attractions, like beaches and viewpoints, are free, specialized excursions, such as volcanic tours or stargazing experiences, may carry additional fees. Planning for these activities in advance ensures that budget expectations align with the experiences desired.

Currency exchange is generally straightforward on La Palma, with banks, exchange offices, and some hotels offering services. However, exchange rates may vary, and fees can apply, so comparing options and planning ahead is wise. Using ATMs or card payments often provides competitive exchange rates, while carrying a small amount of cash in Euros ensures smooth transactions in markets, rural areas, or for minor expenses.

Ultimately, understanding money matters on La Palma empowers travelers to make informed choices, enjoy the island fully, and avoid financial stress. By preparing for cash needs, leveraging cards wisely, budgeting for food, transport, and activities, and planning for shopping and excursions, visitors can maximize their experience without compromise. Effective money management transforms a visit to La Palma into a seamless, relaxed journey where the focus remains on exploring the island's natural beauty, cultural richness, and unique adventures rather than worrying about finances.

Travel Essentials

Traveling to La Palma is a remarkable experience, and preparing the right essentials ensures that every moment is enjoyed fully and comfortably. From packing wisely and understanding local conditions to having the right tools and documents on hand, being well-prepared allows travelers to navigate the island with ease and confidence. Travel essentials extend beyond clothing and luggage—they encompass items, knowledge, and planning strategies that make a trip safer, smoother, and more immersive.

Clothing and footwear are among the most important considerations when packing for La Palma. The island's climate is generally mild, but microclimates can vary dramatically depending on altitude and location. Lightweight clothing is suitable for coastal and lower elevation areas, while warmer layers, rain jackets, and sturdy hiking boots are essential for exploring higher altitudes, forests, and volcanic trails. Breathable fabrics, sun hats, and sunglasses are recommended for daytime excursions, while evening wear should accommodate cooler temperatures in mountainous areas or during coastal breezes. Versatile clothing that can be layered ensures comfort across the island's diverse environments.

Hiking and adventure gear are critical for those planning to explore La Palma's trails, viewpoints, and natural parks. Essentials include a durable backpack, sufficient water, energy snacks, sunscreen, and a first aid kit. Maps, a compass, or a GPS device are useful for navigating less-traveled paths, and trekking poles can provide extra stability on uneven terrain. For those engaging in water sports, equipment such as wetsuits, snorkels, or life jackets enhances both safety and enjoyment. Having the appropriate gear allows travelers to embrace the island's adventurous offerings confidently.

Travel documentation and money management are fundamental essentials. Passports, identification, and any necessary visas should be current and stored securely. Copies of important documents, both digital and physical, provide backups in case of loss or theft. In addition, travelers should carry sufficient cash, credit or debit cards, and a travel wallet for organized access to funds. Knowing the location of ATMs, currency exchange offices, and banking services ensures smooth financial management throughout the trip.

Health-related items are equally important. Medications, prescriptions, and personal hygiene items should be packed in adequate quantities. Sunscreen, insect repellent, and hand sanitizers are essential for both comfort and protection. A basic first aid kit, including bandages, antiseptics, and over-the-counter remedies, addresses minor injuries or illnesses encountered during exploration. Being prepared with health essentials ensures travelers can focus on enjoying La Palma without interruption.

Technology and communication tools are vital for both convenience and safety. Smartphones, chargers, power banks, and cameras capture memories and enable navigation, while offline maps and translation apps can be helpful in areas with limited connectivity. Travel adapters are necessary for charging devices, especially for visitors from regions with different plug standards. Staying connected allows for efficient planning, emergency communication, and documentation of experiences.

Personal comfort items, though often overlooked, enhance the quality of travel. Sunglasses, reusable water bottles, travel pillows, and lightweight blankets contribute to a comfortable journey, whether during flights, ferry rides, or long hikes. Small daypacks or crossbody bags are useful for carrying essentials during excursions, while protective cases for electronics safeguard valuable devices from dust, moisture, or impact. Paying attention to these details ensures a more relaxed and enjoyable experience.

Guides, maps, and local information are indispensable travel essentials. While digital resources are convenient, physical maps, guidebooks, and brochures provide context, historical background, and route options that enhance exploration. Understanding local customs, cultural norms, and emergency contact information ensures responsible and safe travel, as well as meaningful engagement with the communities visited. Knowledgeable preparation empowers travelers to navigate La Palma confidently and respectfully.

For families traveling with children, specific essentials such as snacks, entertainment, and safety equipment are crucial. Strollers, carriers, or child-specific hiking gear make excursions more manageable, while educational resources or activity kits keep children engaged during downtime. Ensuring that children's needs are anticipated and addressed allows the entire family to experience the island comfortably and enjoyably.

Ultimately, having the right travel essentials transforms a trip to La Palma into a seamless, stress-free adventure. Proper clothing, footwear, gear, documentation, health supplies, technology, and comfort items prepare travelers for the island's varied environments and activities. By equipping themselves with these essentials, visitors can focus on exploring La Palma's natural beauty, cultural richness, and hidden treasures, making the journey both safe and unforgettable. Thoughtful preparation enhances the travel experience, turning potential challenges into opportunities for discovery and enjoyment.

Chapter 11

Saying Goodbye

Last Experiences

As a journey to La Palma nears its end, savoring the final experiences of the trip becomes a meaningful way to leave the island with lasting memories. These last experiences are more than a simple conclusion to sightseeing; they offer an opportunity to reflect on the journey, immerse in the culture one final time, and capture moments that will linger long after departure. Being intentional about the final days or hours ensures that travelers depart with a sense of fulfillment, appreciation, and connection to the island.

One of the most rewarding last experiences is revisiting favorite spots or hidden gems discovered earlier in the trip. Perhaps it is a secluded viewpoint overlooking the Atlantic Ocean, a quiet black sand beach, or a charming village square where local life unfolds at its own pace. Returning to these locations allows travelers to savor the atmosphere, take additional photographs, or simply absorb the sensory richness of the place. These revisits provide a final opportunity to connect with the landscape and people, reinforcing memories that might otherwise fade with time.

Culinary experiences are another essential part of last moments on La Palma. A farewell meal at a beloved local restaurant or a casual café can highlight the island's diverse flavors one last time. Sampling regional specialties such as fresh seafood, papas arrugadas with mojo sauces, or traditional desserts offers a multisensory experience that encapsulates the essence of La Palma. Visiting a local market one final time to pick up specialty foods, snacks, or ingredients to take home allows travelers to carry a piece of the island's culture beyond its shores.

Cultural engagement during these final experiences deepens the sense of connection to La Palma. Attending a local festival, music performance, or artisanal workshop provides insight into traditions that define the island's identity. Travelers may choose to participate in a dance, craft a small souvenir, or engage in conversations with local residents. These experiences foster understanding, appreciation, and interaction, leaving a lasting impression of La Palma as a living, vibrant community rather than just a scenic destination.

For those who love adventure, fitting in a last activity such as a short hike, a kayaking excursion, or a stargazing session ensures that the island's natural beauty is appreciated to the fullest. These final adventures can be tailored to individual energy levels and interests, providing a satisfying conclusion to active exploration. Experiencing the volcanic landscapes, lush forests, or serene coastlines one last time reinforces the island's diversity and majesty in the traveler's memory.

Photography and journaling during these last experiences help capture the emotional and visual essence of the journey. Revisiting favorite spots with the perspective of having explored the island in depth allows travelers to notice details previously overlooked. Whether it's a sunset over a volcanic ridge, the intricate architecture of a historic church, or the vibrant colors of a local market, recording these moments ensures that the impressions remain vivid long after returning home. Journaling reflections, thoughts, and personal stories adds a narrative layer to the memories, creating a meaningful keepsake.

A final walk through a town or village offers a chance to observe daily life, interact with locals, and reflect on the rhythm of the island. Observing children playing in the streets, neighbors greeting each other, and market vendors packing up their goods provides a snapshot of La Palma's authentic culture. These ordinary moments often leave a stronger emotional impact than grand tourist attractions, reminding travelers of the human connections and small pleasures that define the island experience.

Taking time for personal reflection is an important part of last experiences. Pausing at a favorite spot to watch the ocean, mountains, or sunset allows travelers to internalize the journey's significance. Reflecting on new discoveries, cultural insights, and personal growth achieved during the trip creates a sense of closure and gratitude. These moments of contemplation transform the final days into an emotional and meaningful part of the travel experience.

Souvenir collection during the last experiences offers practical ways to remember the trip. Whether purchasing handmade crafts, locally produced foods, or small tokens from markets and boutiques, travelers can choose items that hold personal significance. Selecting souvenirs with care, guided by memories and stories from the journey, ensures that these mementos serve as tangible reminders of La Palma's landscapes, culture, and people.

Ultimately, last experiences on La Palma are about savoring the island one final time, engaging fully with its culture, nature, and community. By revisiting favorite spots, enjoying culinary delights, participating in cultural activities, embarking on a final adventure, and reflecting on the journey, travelers can leave with a deep sense of connection and satisfaction. These moments create enduring memories that carry the spirit of La Palma home, allowing the magic of the island to remain with visitors long after their departure.

Capturing Memories

One of the most treasured aspects of traveling to La Palma is the ability to capture memories that will last a lifetime. The island's dramatic landscapes, lush forests, volcanic craters, charming villages, and vibrant local life provide endless opportunities to document experiences in meaningful ways. Capturing memories goes beyond simple photographs; it encompasses journaling, sketches, videos, and even collecting small keepsakes, all of which help travelers relive their journey long after they have left the island.

Photography is often the primary method for preserving memories on La Palma. From the rugged volcanic coastlines and black sand beaches to the verdant laurel forests and panoramic viewpoints, every corner of the island offers breathtaking scenes. Capturing sunrise and sunset over the mountains or the ocean provides a sense of time and atmosphere, while candid shots of village life convey the warmth and character of local communities. Travelers are encouraged to explore both popular landmarks and lesser-known spots, as off-the-beaten-path locations often yield the most unique and personal images.

Journaling is another powerful tool for memory preservation. Recording thoughts, emotions, and experiences in a dedicated travel journal allows visitors to reflect on their journey in a deeper and more personal way. Entries can include descriptions of encounters with locals, the taste of a favorite dish, the challenge of a hiking trail, or the serenity of a secluded beach. Including sketches, pressed flowers, or ticket stubs enhances the narrative and transforms a simple journal into a tangible diary of the trip. This practice not only captures the facts of the journey but also the feelings and impressions that make the experience unforgettable.

Videos provide a dynamic and immersive way to capture La Palma's energy. Short clips of waves crashing against cliffs, the rustling of leaves in laurel forests, or the bustle of local markets allow travelers to revisit the sounds, movements, and atmospheres of the island. Recording interactions with locals, participation in festivals, or moments of adventure such as hiking or kayaking creates a living record of experiences. Videos offer a sense of presence that static photographs cannot, helping travelers relive the vibrancy of the island whenever they wish.

Collecting small keepsakes adds a tangible dimension to memories. Items such as seashells, handmade crafts, postcards, or locally produced foods serve as reminders of specific places and experiences. Each object tells a story, whether it is a piece of volcanic stone from a crater hike or a handcrafted ornament from a village market. Keepsakes, when thoughtfully selected and preserved, provide a sensory connection to La Palma that complements visual and written documentation.

Maps and itineraries also play a role in capturing memories. Marking visited trails, viewpoints, villages, and attractions on a map creates a visual record of the journey. Travelers can annotate routes with notes about what they saw, tasted, or felt in each location. This practice transforms a simple navigation tool into a personalized memory map, providing context and continuity that enhances reflection long after the trip ends.

Engaging with locals and capturing their stories enriches the memory-keeping process. Recording anecdotes, interviews, or conversations allows travelers to preserve the human side of La Palma's culture. These narratives provide insight into traditions, daily life, and community values, creating a multidimensional memory of the island that goes beyond landscapes and landmarks. Sharing these stories with friends, family, or even through blogs and social media can extend the impact of the travel experience.

Creative expressions such as sketches, paintings, or scrapbooks offer artistic ways to preserve memories. Travelers who enjoy drawing or crafting can incorporate observations from nature, architecture, and daily life into visual representations. These personalized creations become unique souvenirs, reflecting not only the island's beauty but also the traveler's perspective and creativity. They serve as both a reminder of the trip and a personal artistic achievement inspired by La Palma.

Organizing and curating memories is equally important. Creating photo albums, digital slideshows, or memory boxes allows travelers to revisit their experiences in an organized and meaningful way. Adding captions, dates, and personal reflections enhances the narrative, transforming collected materials into a story of the journey. This curation process helps preserve the richness and diversity of experiences, ensuring that memories remain vivid and accessible.

Ultimately, capturing memories on La Palma is about more than recording images or collecting items—it is about preserving the essence of the island and the personal experiences it evokes. By combining photography, journaling, videos, keepsakes, storytelling, and creative expression, travelers create a multifaceted record of their journey. These memories serve as a lasting connection to La Palma, allowing the beauty, culture, and spirit of the island to continue inspiring and enriching visitors long after they return home.

Planning Your Return

As a journey on La Palma comes to a close, careful planning for the return home is essential to ensure that the final phase of the trip is smooth, stress-free, and leaves travelers with lasting positive memories. Planning a return is more than simply booking transportation—it involves organizing logistics, managing time efficiently, safeguarding belongings, and reflecting on the experiences gained during the stay. Thoughtful preparation for departure allows visitors to leave the island with a sense of closure and satisfaction.

One of the first considerations is scheduling transportation. La Palma is served by both its international airport and ferry connections to other Canary Islands. Booking flights or ferry tickets in advance ensures availability and often provides better pricing. Travelers should allow adequate time for check-in, security, and potential delays, particularly if returning during busy tourist seasons. Coordinating ground transportation from accommodations to ports or airports is equally important; pre-arranged taxis, shuttle services, or car rentals can prevent last-minute stress and ensure timely arrival.

Packing is another crucial step in planning the return. Carefully reviewing belongings prevents leaving valuable items behind and ensures that souvenirs, gifts, and personal items are properly secured for transport. Using durable luggage, protective covers for fragile items, and appropriate organization techniques minimizes the risk of damage or loss. Travel regulations regarding liquids, food products, and other restricted items should be checked in advance to avoid complications during airport or ferry inspections. Thoughtful packing contributes to a smoother departure and allows travelers to focus on enjoying the final moments on the island.

Managing finances is an important aspect of the return process. Settling outstanding bills at hotels, restaurants, or transportation providers avoids surprises during checkout. Converting leftover local currency or withdrawing funds for final expenses ensures that no financial obligations are left unmanaged. Travelers should also verify that credit cards and payment methods are functioning correctly for any last-minute transactions. Efficient money management provides peace of mind and prevents unnecessary stress at the end of the trip.

Health and safety considerations remain relevant during the return. Ensuring that medications, personal hygiene items, and travel documents are readily accessible during travel helps avoid last-minute complications. Having a small travel kit with essentials such as snacks, water, and comfort items for the journey makes the return more pleasant, particularly for long flights or ferry rides. Being mindful of fatigue, hydration, and nutrition ensures that travelers arrive home in good condition and ready to transition back to daily life.

Reflecting on experiences during the final days enhances the emotional closure of the trip. Taking time to revisit favorite spots, savor local cuisine one last time, or interact with locals allows travelers to solidify memories before departure. Writing in a journal, taking final photographs, or creating small mementos reinforces the connection to the island and captures the essence of the journey. These reflective activities provide a sense of completion and personal fulfillment.

Communicating with hosts, local contacts, or tour providers is also part of planning the return. Expressing gratitude for hospitality, confirming final arrangements, and coordinating pickups or checkouts strengthens positive relationships and ensures a seamless conclusion to services used. Such interactions reflect respect for the local community and leave a favorable impression, creating goodwill for potential future visits.

Travelers should also consider logistical preparations upon returning home. Arranging airport transfers, notifying family or friends of arrival times, and confirming onward travel plans ensures a smooth transition. For international travelers, understanding customs procedures, baggage regulations, and entry requirements in their home country prevents delays and complications. Preparing these details in advance contributes to a stress-free return journey.

Finally, planning the return includes taking care of emotional and mental transitions. Traveling can be immersive, and leaving an island like La Palma may evoke a mix of nostalgia and anticipation. Setting aside time to mentally process the experiences, organize photographs and souvenirs, and reflect on personal growth helps travelers integrate the journey into their broader life narrative. Recognizing the impact of the trip and expressing gratitude for the experiences ensures that the memories remain vivid and meaningful.

Ultimately, planning the return from La Palma is about balancing practical logistics with personal reflection. From transportation and packing to financial management, health considerations, and emotional closure, careful preparation ensures that the final moments on the island are as rewarding as the first. By approaching departure thoughtfully, travelers can leave La Palma with a sense of completion, cherished memories, and a readiness to carry the spirit of the island into everyday life, making the journey truly unforgettable.

Printed in Dunstable, United Kingdom